Hope & Help
For The Single Mom

The

21 Principles

Of a

Healthy Single Mom

Published by Lori Little
Atlanta, Georgia

To my son Eric,
There are no words to describe how much I love you and cherish every moment that I am blessed to spend with you. I am so proud of the fine young man that you have become. Thank you for being such an amazing son. You make me want to be a better mom.

To my dear friends Bob and Marilyn,
Thank you for the blessing that you are in my life and for the way you have poured into me. You are a true example of what real friends are.

Contents

Lori became a single mom when her son Eric was just eighteen months old, and is still a single mother today. Her back ground was in corporate business development and sales, and she was the original Director of **John Maxwell's** Thrive! More important though Lori has the understanding and commitment gained from thirteen years of single motherhood.

Please visit the website to learn more about Lori and her "21 Principles of a Healthy Single Mom" at **www.hope4singlemoms.com**

Copyright © 2010
Lori Little
ISBN: 978-0-578-07995-0

Printed in US by Instantpublisher.com

All Scripture from the New American Standard Bible and the New International Bible.

PART 1

PURPOSE AND MEANING

ACCESS TO THE 21 PRINCIPLES RESOURCES

1. Every 21 Principles Book comes with Resources to hold a 21 Principles Small Group. For access to downloadable Posters, Invitations, Bulletin Inserts, Diploma for each graduate and Workbook for Principles 1 and 3 please send an email to: bookresources@hope4singlemoms.com

2. Every 21 Principles Book comes with access to the 21 Principles Audio Interviews to listen to after reading each Principle. For access to the 21 Principles Interviews please send an email to: bookdownloads@hope4singlemoms.com

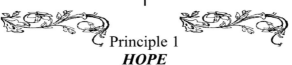

Principle 1
HOPE

"For there is hope for a tree, when it is cut down, that it will sprout again, and its shoots will not fail. Though its roots grow old in the ground and its stump dies in the dry soil, at the scent of water it will flourish and put forth sprigs like a plant." Job 14:7-9

It was a terrible, cold, lonely night in October of 1998 when I hit rock bottom. It was the night I gave up hope in being a single mom. If there were wrong roads to travel down, I went down them. If there were mistakes to be made, I made them. It seemed that I had exhausted all of my efforts to find some hope and peace in this crazy situation of single motherhood. I looked everywhere; everywhere except to God.

At first, I put my hope in finding a new husband for me and a father for my son. After the first relationship failed, I went further into depression. Then another love came along, and that failed too. Time after time every relationship failed.

Next I tried putting my hope in my finances. I thought that everything would be just grand if I could stay in my nice, upscale neighborhood. It was difficult to hold down a job though, for I was an emotional wreck, and constantly exhausted. Putting my hope in finances failed me too. As you know, it takes a lot of money to pay for everything that you need. It was so much more than I could manage on my own.

I also tried putting my hope in other people, and that failed me too. My married friends stopped hanging out with me, or inviting me over. I also felt like I did not fit in at my church anymore, so I just stopped going. I became totally isolated, and even more depressed.

Then I made the horrible mistake of putting my hope in my son. I thought if everything else failed me that surely I could find my hope in him. I quickly learned how selfish that was to lean on a child like that. We need to pour our heart and energy into our children, but they cannot be our source of hope.

On that lonesome October night, I fell to my knees and cried out to God for help. I told him that he needed to show up or I was checking out. I could not do this single mom life anymore. The moment I called His name the God of the universe paused just for me and said, "Here I am. I've been here with you all along. I was just waiting to hear from you." For the first time, I felt God's presence with me and His arms of love surrounding me. Then I heard the Lord whisper in my spirit, "Don't you give up Lori. Don't you quit; you be strong. You have a son that needs you and I have great plans for your life." I could not understand what I just heard. Was that God or just my messed up mind hearing things?

Suddenly I recalled the verse a client of mine had in a frame on her desk. It was Jeremiah 29:11 that said, **"For I know the plans I have for you, plans to prosper you, not to harm you; plans to give you hope and a future."** I was delighted that verse was somehow tucked away in my memory. Unfortunately, that was the extent of my Bible knowledge.

I finally felt that I had something concrete to put my hope in now. I spent the rest of the night nestled in the arms of God weeping. There was an enormous sense of peace within me now. I knew that God was real and that somehow everything was going to be okay.

The next day I bought my first Bible. Any extra time I had was devoted to reading God's word. The more I read about God, the closer I felt to Him. Hope and joy started stirring up inside of me, even though my situation had not changed.

Over the passage of time, the Lord showed me twenty one verses to follow. He promised me that if I followed them I would live in victory as a single mom. They are now what you are reading the, "21 Principles of a Healthy Single Mom." You too will live in victory if you use them in your life.

Ever since that dark October night I fell in love with the word hope. It encouraged me to hold on for something better than this life offered. According to Webster's Dictionary, the word hope means, "To wish for something with the expectation of its fulfillment. To have confidence, or trust. To look forward to with confidence or expectation, one that is a source of or reason for hope." Jesus Christ is now my source and reason for hope as a single mom.

Here is a wonderful verse the Lord showed me about hope. It is from Job 14: 7-9 that says, **"For there is hope for a tree when it is cut down, that it will sprout again, and its shoots will not fail. Though its roots grow old in the ground and its stump dies in the dry soil, at the scent of water it will flourish and put forth sprigs like a plant."**

Maybe you think that life has cut you down like that tree. Possibly you feel like you are dying and withering away as a single mom. I am here to say to you today, "Don't give up, don't quit. One moment in the presence of God and one drop of His living water will change your life forever." When you put your hope in Jesus, you will flourish as a single mom. He will help you live a life of purpose and meaning, focus and order, balance and harmony.

If you feel you want to give up, please know that you are not alone. I wanted to at one time, and I know of so many other single moms that have felt the same way. It may help you to know that even people in the Bible felt like that. Here is what Job said in 6: 8 – 9, **"Oh that my request might come to pass and that God would grant my longing! Would that God were willing to crush me, that He would loose His hand and cut me off!"** Job just wanted to die, so he could be free from all of his pain and suffering.

God did not grant Job his request, nor mine or yours if you asked him. He has a greater way for you than that because God is a good God. You may wonder, "So what should a single mom do when she has lost all hope in everything this world has to offer?" The Bible says in First Timothy 5:5, **"The widow who is really in need and left all alone puts her hope in God and continues night and day to pray and to ask God for help."**

My desire for you in this Principle is to apply the verse of Jeremiah 29:11 to your life. The first sentence we will start with says, "For I know the plans I have for you." Who do you think "I" is in this verse? It is God of course. The next issue we need to address is, "Who is God to us?" He is our Heavenly Father; our Abba, Father and Daddy. In this world, we have a Heavenly Father and an earthy father. When the disciples asked Jesus to teach them how to pray in Matthew 6:9, Jesus started his prayer in this way, "Our Father." Jesus also referred to God as, "Abba" which means "Father" as Mark 14:36 says, **"And he was saying, Abba! Father! All things are possible for you; remove this cup from me; yet not what I will, but what you will."**

As I mentioned earlier, you have two fathers; a Heavenly Father and a human father. Your earthly father did not make you. Yes, your earthly parents conceived you but they are not who made you. God made you as His word says in Psalm 139:13-14, **"For you created my inmost**

being; you knit me together in my mother's womb. I praise you because I am fearfully and wonderfully made! Your works are wonderful." Can you believe that God made you for His purpose and joy? I wonder how many of us single moms can wake up every morning and say to God, "Thank you for making me. I am wonderful and beautiful because you made me for your purpose and pleasure." I know I could not say that when I first heard this verse.

Seeing God as our Father does not sit too well with some of us single mothers. *We perceive what God is like by the way important people in our lives have failed us or mistreated us.* That can represent your child's father, parents, family members, friends, husbands, or boyfriends. Possibly you went through some extremely difficult things when you were a child that hurt you. Maybe it was a controlling parent, a weak father, verbal, emotional, physical abuse or parental neglect.

Unfortunately, so many children grow up with severe rejection from their parents that leaves them feeling unwanted by them or God. Maybe some of the important people in your life nit-picked at you and wanted you to do everything right. Possibly they were unforgiving, cold, demanding, insensitive, uncaring, angry or cruel to you.

For example, a weak father figure in your life can cause you to look for love in all the wrong places. We make other men our knight in shinning armor because we were left unprotected, neglected or uncared for. The image we have of God is formed at an unusually young age.

I did not know the truth of God's word as a child or when I first became a single mom. It was difficult for me to realize that God loves me unconditionally. I questioned how he would protect us, and I doubted that he wanted the best for my son and me. For whatever reason your child's father is no longer with you, it can be difficult to understand as a single mom that God is your husband. His word says in Isaiah 54:5, **"For the Lord your God is your husband – the Lord Almighty is his name."** It may also be difficult to understand Deuteronomy 31:8 that says, **"The Lord himself goes before you and will be with you; he will never leave you nor forsake you."** With our children not having a father in the house it can be difficult for us, and them, to see God as their father. His word says in Psalm 68:5 He is, **"A father to the fatherless, a defender of widows, is God in his holy dwelling place."**

The truth about God is that he is never mean, cruel or abusive to us. People do those kinds of things to each other. It is crucial to believe that God made you for his pleasure. Real love comes from the way God loves you, sees you and treats you. Not what other people have done to you, even though those things hurt.

God is a good God, and he is all about hope not hopelessness. His desire for you on this earth is to live in what His Kingdom is all about; righteousness, peace and joy. Reading the Bible is the best tool you have to learn about God. It is life and truth, and if whatever you are thinking or feeling is not in there then it is a lie.

For example, maybe you believe the lie that God does not think that you are someone remarkable. Possibly your mom, dad, boyfriend or husband did not treat you that way. God thinks you are absolutely incredible. His word says so in Deuteronomy 32:9-10, **"I am the apple of His eye."**

I have discovered from reading my Bible that God is kind and compassionate. He accepts me, loves me and longs to be with me. One Bible translation says that God "yearns" to be with me. He is patient, kind, gentle, and full of grace and mercy towards me. I am the apple of His eye no matter what I have done. When you use your time to read the

Bible on your own, you will see that God is a good God. He truly wants nothing but the best for you and your children. My Bible does not say that God hates me or that he is out to get me. God does not think I am a looser as a single mom. I invite you to discover this truth for yourself. Here is some basic theology that may help you better understand that God is a good God to single mothers.

1. God is an *Omnipotent* God which means He has absolute power. God can do anything including bringing you through this single mom life victoriously. We have some power, the enemy has some power but God is power!

2. God is an *Omnipresence* God which means that His presence is everywhere. There is no spot in this world you can go that God will not be there with you. This should provide comfort and safety to you as a single mom to know that you are never alone.

3. God is an *Omniscient* God which means that he has full knowledge of everything. This should prevent any confusion or concern about your future. God has an incredible plan for you even if you do not have one for yourself. His plan for you is good because God is a good God. He knows everything that has ever gone on with you. God can see behind the mask, and he still loves you. That is why you can put all of your hope and trust in Him as a single mom. Hope in people and things cause death and hopelessness. Hope in God brings life and happiness.

 You are a winner with God. You can get through this time in your life, and remember it is a season, and it will pass. God can make you healthy in every sector of your life; spiritually, emotionally, mentally, physically, financially and socially. He can instruct you how to balance your life, family, home and career. He can also help you raise healthy children.

My prayer is that you experience the life that God intended for you. A life filled with purpose and meaning, focus and order, balance and harmony. This can only be achieved by the Holy Spirit working in and through you. I pray that today is the time you will put your hope in God. Let Him lift you up on eagles' wings, so both you and your children can soar to a new life with Him.

Questions:
1. We tend to view what God is like based off of the way people have failed us or mistreated us. How has your view of God changed by realizing this?
2. What plan can you implement into your life to learn more about God?
3. What things besides Jesus have you put your hope in?
4. What changes do you have to make to now put all of your hope in Jesus?

Go through Section One of the downloadable Workbook. To access the Workbook send an email to: bookresources@hope4singlemoms.com

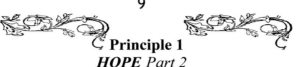

Principle 1
HOPE Part 2

The second part of our verse in Jeremiah 29:11 says, **"My plans are to prosper you."** Do you believe that it is God's will to prosper you as a single mom? I admit I did not believe that when I first heard it. Because of the shame and guilt deep inside of me, I did not believe that God's prosperity was for me. Again, I believed a lie. No where in my Bible does it say that God does not want me to prosper.

What most of us do not realize is that there is a vast difference between the words prosper, prosperity and prosperous. The word prosperity means wealth and success while the word prosperous means to succeed. The word prosper means to flourish, bloom or to be in your prime season.

This definition of God's plan to prosper you is best found in 3 John 1:2 that says, **"Beloved, I pray that in all respects you may prosper and be in good health, just as your soul prospers."** What I find intriguing about this verse is that God does not mention anything about money. Many single moms tend to think to prosper is all about finances. God is concerned about your finances, soul and body. In this chapter you will discover God's plan for your soul to prosper; or what inner prosperity means.

There are five scriptures about inner prosperity we will use in this part of the Principle of Hope.

1. The first is Genesis 32:12 that says, **"I will surely prosper you and make your descendants as the sand of the sea, which is too great to be numbered."**

God is saying that for you and your children to prosper all stands on your relationship with Him. In this verse God is saying, "Get to know me. Get into my word and be in prayer daily with me." In the book of Hosea God's word says, **"My people are destroyed for lack of knowledge."** In order to prosper as a single mom, you have to daily spend time in prayer and reading God's word. It is also advantageous to fast during the time that you need to hear from God. You are in charge of raising a future generation and it is your responsibility to put the word of God into your children. We cannot impart what we do not know, so read God's word for yourself and then read it to your children. Remember also to pray daily on your own and with them. God can turn any situation around, but most of all when you read and pray God changes you.

 2. The second verse God shows us is 1Samuel 18:24 that says, **"David was prospering in all his ways for the Lord was with him."**

When you put God at the center of every detail and circumstances of your life He will honor what you are doing. Everything that we do must be consecrated to God, meaning to dedicate it to God and give it to Him first before you do it. We are to "Seek first His Kingdom" for life here on earth is about being in God's will and not our own.

3. The third verse God shows us is 2 Chronicles 14: 7 that says, **"For he said to Judah, "Let us build these cities and surround them with walls and towers, gates and bars. The land is still ours because we have sought the Lord our God; we have sought Him and He has given us rest on every side. So they built and prospered."**

The analogy that I feel led to use here is how to build a house. What is the first part of the house that you build? It is the foundation; the basis on which the entire house stands. Our foundation needs to be the word of God, and the building must first start in our mind. We need to ask our selves, "Do I believe the truth of God's word? Or, do I believe the world's lie?" The lies must be erased, and our minds need to be reprogrammed with the truth of God's word. This is what Paul meant in Romans 12:2 when he said, **"And do not be conformed to the world, but be transformed by the renewing of your mind, so that you may prove what the will of God is, that which is good and acceptable and perfect."**

Filling your mind with truth prepares you for battling the enemy's lies. The enemy will whisper in your ear how unloved you are because you do not have a husband. With your renewed mind and firm foundation you battle back saying Isaiah 54:5, **"Your husband is your maker. The Lord Almighty is His name."** The enemy will try to tell you that you can not do this single mom life. With a renewed mind and firm foundation you battle back saying Philippians 4:13, **"I can do all things in Gods will through Christ who strengthens me."** The enemy will also try to tell you that you are nothing; you are just a single mom. With a renewed mind and firm foundation you battle back saying 1Peter 2:9, **"I am a chosen race, a royal priesthood, a Holy Nation, a people for God's own possession."**

The book, "The Art of War" is a classic on achieving victory on the battlefield. It says, "If you know the enemy and know yourself, you need not fear the result of a hundred battles. If you know yourself but not the enemy, for every victory gained, you will also suffer a defeat. If you know neither the enemy nor yourself, you will lose in every battle." Build your foundation and walls off of God's truth and not the world's lies. God's word is rest and peace for the soul.

4. The fourth scripture God gives us is Psalms10: 5 that says, **"His ways prosper at all times; your judgments are on high, out of his sight; As for all his adversaries, he snorts at them."**
Have you ever wondered why wicked people get so wealthy or succeed at everything they do? How about the way they brag how they did it on their own and that God had nothing to do with it? All while we are striving to do the right thing, and sometimes barely have enough food to eat.   Remember that wealth is only temporary and not a sign of Gods approval, nor is the lack of it a sign of God's disapproval. God hates evil, and these people will not go unpunished. I heard a story about a rich man who was asked how much money is enough. He replied, "A little bit more." To desire more of earth's treasures and pleasures goes against God's request to, "Seek first the kingdom." When you are not thankful or grateful for what you have it is a sure sign that your heart is far away from God.

5. The last verse God gives us about how to flourish or prosper is from Psalm 122:6 that says, **"Pray for the peace of Jerusalem, may they prosper who love you."**
Here the psalmist was not praying for his own peace and prosperity, he was praying for others. Did you know that we prosper when we pray for other people? This is what intercessory pray is about; standing in the gap for others. God works on this earth through humans, and he needs us to pray for others. Paul often asks others to pray for him through out his writings as stated in 2Thes 3:1, **"Finally, brethren, pray for us that the word of the Lord will spread rapidly and be glorified, just as it did also with you."** When we pray we have peace within our selves about our own needs, and we can release that peace to others through intercession.

The apostle Paul set the greatest example of what it means for our soul to prosper in Philippians 4:12 that says, **"I know how to get along with humble means, and I also know how to live in prosperity; in any and every circumstance I have learned the secret of being filled and going hungry, both of having abundance and suffering need."** Paul had his priorities straight here, for he was thankful and grateful for everything that God had given him; no matter how much or how little.

Paul's secret to contentment, and ours too, is to trust God that He is who he says He is. We need to rely on God's power and strength, not our own. Paul focused on what he should be doing instead of what he did not have. Sometimes it is beneficial for us not to have all of the material things we desire. Often our desire for more is just a longing to fill a void in our life.

The last part of our verse in Jeremiah 29:11 says, **"My plans are not to harm you. My plans are to give you hope and a future."** If you do not have a close relationship with Christ it may be easy to think that God is out to get you. Or, that he just wants to beat you up and make your life miserable. I cannot find anywhere in my Bible where it says that. God loves us no matter what we have done or what sin we have committed. It is because of His unconditional love that He sent his only son to die on the cross for us. God's only son took that beating for us over two thousand years ago, so we can have eternal life with him.

God's kingdom is about righteousness, peace and joy. He wants your life filled with the fruits of the Holy Spirit which are; love, joy, peace, patience, kindness, goodness, faithfulness, gentleness and self control. God's plan is not for us to be depressed and ready to give up. God sent His son, Jesus Christ, to die for us so we can have life abundantly. That means heaven is right here on earth with a personal relationship with Jesus.

When we can grasp this Principle of Hope the verses of Jeremiah 29:12-14 will come alive for you. They say, **"Then you will call upon me and come and pray to me and I will listen to you. You will seek me and find me when you search for me with all your heart. I will be found by you, declares the Lord and I will restore your fortunes and will gather you from all the nations and from all the places where I have driven you declares the Lord and I will bring you back from the place of captivity."**

In these verses God did not forget about His people even though they were in captivity. He has not forgotten about you in these times of struggles and trials as a single mom. God planned to give His people a new beginning with a new purpose; to turn them into new people. God is preparing you to be a healthy single mom with Him at the center of your life. That my dear single mom is what hope is all about. I invite you today to make Jesus Christ your one and only source and reason for hope.

Questions:
1. What areas of your life are you claiming as your own and not letting God into? What do you think would happen if you let God have control of these areas?
2. How strong is your foundation? In what areas do you need to renew your mind?
3. What is taking priority over God in your life? Why are these things more important to you than God?
4. Who do you know that needs a release of peace that you can pray for?

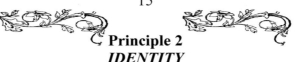

Principle 2
IDENTITY

"While he was still speaking, a bright cloud overshadowed them, and behold, a voice out of the cloud said, "This is my beloved Son, with whom I am well-pleased; listen to Him." Matthew 17:5

Becoming a single mom felt like moving to a different planet. Everything seemed so strange and totally out of place from the life I once knew. I was lost, and had no concept of who I was anymore. When I looked in the mirror I saw a strange new reflection staring back. I constantly asked myself, "Who am I as a single mom now?"

If you were once married and now divorced or widowed, your entire identity may have been based off of being a wife. You may wonder, "Who am I now that I do not have the role or title of wife anymore?" Maybe you are a teenager or have never been married before, and now you find your self in a new role; single motherhood. Just because your position, role, title or marital status changed, nothing has changed about who you are.

One of the greatest questions ever presented to me was from Dr. Charles Stanley. We went into his office to speak for a while before going into the recording studio. He looked at me from across his desk and said, "Lori, tell me about who you are?"

What a fascinating question. There were several choices that I briefly considered telling him about who I was. I could have said that I am the author of the 21 Principles, a speaker, founder of Hope and Help for the Single Mom or Eric's mom. What would you have said? How would you respond to the question, "Tell me about who you are?"

If I answered Dr. Stanley by saying that I was Lori Little that would have been telling him my name. If I said I was an author and speaker that would have been telling him what I do. If I said I was a single mother that would have been telling him my marital and parental status.

I did not want to tell him how I used to think of myself as a single mom; a total looser. I put on that "Scarlet D" and labeled myself as divorced. Some of us have been divorced more than once, so we add more "Scarlet D's" to our titles. I was merely exchanging one false title for another. I took off the false title of Mrs. and wife, and exchanged it for baggage, unwanted, rejected, ugly, fat, shame, guilt, package deal, insecure and insignificant. I thought that the titles I wore reflected who I truly was. I hated myself more and more with every false title I added. I could not even look in the mirror without being disgusted at what I saw. I remember not even being able to look at a picture of myself without finding fault or cutting myself down.

The more I hated myself the more withdrawn and isolated I became. I just wanted to lock myself up and hide from everyone. I even tried to hide from God. I also disconnected myself from my family, friends and church.

I remember one particularly lonely night I felt a nudge in my Spirit to read the beginning of Genesis. When I got to 3:8-11, the verses hit me like a ton of bricks. They said, **"They (meaning Adam and Eve) heard the sound of the Lord God walking in the garden in the cool of the day, and the man and his wife hid themselves from the presence of the Lord God among the trees of the garden. Then the Lord God called to the man, and said to him, "Where are you?" He said, "I heard the sound of you in the garden, and I was afraid because I was naked; so I hid myself. And He (God) said, "Who told you that you were naked?"**

I immediately felt the Holy Spirit ask me, *"Who told you that you are a looser? Who told you that you and your child are a package deal? Who told you that you are rejected? Who told you that you are unwanted or insignificant? That is not the way that I see you.*" I had to ask myself, "Who did tell me all of those things?" I came to realize that I brought a lot of those things on myself and accepted what other people said about me as truth. I also learned that Satan whispered a bunch of lies to me that I bought right into.

I started thinking about some of things that happened to me when I was just a young girl. I recalled some of the unpleasant things that happened, and the terrible names I was called. What hurt me the most however were the sins that I brought into my own life as I became older, especially with men. I got involved with them because I felt so empty on the inside.

What I have learned is that my *feelings* caused the false labels. My husband left me, so I *felt* rejected and unloved. He left me for another woman which made me *feel* like a piece of trash. I *felt* awful from all the offensive names I was once called. Because I *felt* like a divorced looser, I acted like a divorced looser. Because I *felt* like a piece of trash, I acted like a piece of trash. I hated myself. I remember thinking, "Who is ever going to love me? I have all this baggage, and I'm a divorced looser with a child." Because I hated myself so much, I lowered my standards in the men I got into relationships with. I did not think I was worthy enough to have anything better come along in my life. It makes me sick to my stomach that I ever once considered my son and myself as a package deal or baggage. What a horrible, horrible lie. I do not know how much cheaper I could get than to believe lies like that. I was letting my *feelings* decide what I thought was the *truth* about myself. The way I *behaved* was based on what I *believed* about myself. Thinking that way is wrong. One of the greatest things I believe I ever heard the Lord speak to my Spirit was when He said, *"Lori, the only person you are is the one that I say you are."*

What changed my life forever was to see myself the way God truly sees me. Because I changed my way of thinking my son changed his way of thinking. Nowhere in my Bible can I find where God says that I am a looser, baggage, unloved and all of the other things I saw myself as.

Let me share with you what I found in my Bible about how God sees me.

I am the apple of God's eye (Deuteronomy 32:9-10)

I am the salt and light of the earth (Matthew 5:13-14)

I am God's child (John 1:12)

I am Christ's friend (John 15:15)

I am a branch of the true vine, a channel of His life (John 15:1, 5)

I have been chosen and appointed to bear fruit (John 15:16)

I am a personal witness of Christ (Acts 1:8)

I have been justified (Romans 3:24)

I am free from condemnation (Romans 8:1, 2)

I am assured that all things work together for my good (Romans 8:28)

I am free from any condemning charges against me (Romans 8:31-34)

I cannot be separated from the love of God (Romans 8:35-39)

I have been sanctified in Christ (1Cornithians 1:2)

I am righteous and holy (1Cornithians 1:30)

I am God's temple (1 Corinthians 3:16)

I am united with the Lord, I am one spirit with Him (1Cornithians 6:17)

I have been bought with a price. I belong to God (1Corinthians 6:20)

I am a member of Christ's Body (1 Corinthians 12:27)

I have been established, anointed and sealed by God (2 Corinthians 1:21, 22)

I am a new creature (2 Corinthians 5:17)

I have received God's righteousness (2 Corinthians 5:21)

I am God's co-worker (2 Corinthians 6:1)

I am one in Christ (Galatians 3:28)

I am a saint (Ephesians 1:1)

I am blessed with every spiritual blessing (Ephesians 1:3)

I am holy, blameless and covered with God's love (Ephesians 1:4)

I have been adopted as God's child (Ephesians 1:5-6)

I am forgiven, and my sins have been taken away (Ephesians 1:7)

I am marked as belonging to God (Ephesians 1:13)

I have been raised up to sit with Christ (Ephesians 2:6)

I am God's work of art (Ephesians 2:10)

I have been brought near to God (Ephesians 2:13)

I have direct access to God through the Holy Spirit (Ephesians 2:18)

I share in the promise of Christ (Ephesians 3:6)

I can come into God's presence with freedom and confidence (Ephesians 3:12)

I am a member of Christ's body (Ephesians 5:29-30)

I am confident that the good work God has begun in me will be perfected (Philippians 1:6)

I am a citizen of Heaven (Philippians 3:20)

I can do all things through Christ who strengthens me (Philippians 4:3)

I have been redeemed and forgiven of all my sins (Colossians 1:14)

I am complete in Christ (Colossians 2:10)

I am set free from my sinful nature (Colossians 2:11)

I am hidden with Christ in God (Colossians 3:3)

I have not been given a spirit of fear, but of power love and a sound mind (2 Timothy 1:7)

I have eternal glory (2 Timothy 2:10)
I can find grace and mercy in time of need (Hebrews 4:16)
I am born of God and the evil one cannot touch me (1 John 5:18)

My first reaction when I read these verses was, "That is the most beautiful thing that I have ever heard about myself." Then along came Satan saying, "Those things are not for you, not with all of the things that you have done in your life." Satan does not want you to understand and trust God's truth about who you are. If you do not believe these verses are true, then you can call God a liar. Remember that Satan is the father of lies, not God.

I had to read these scriptures several times a day for an extraordinarily long time before I started to believe they were all true about me. I had to allow God's word to remove the lies that I once believed, and reprogram my mind with His truth.

You must allow the *truth* of God's word to determine what you *believe* about yourself. Then your belief about yourself will determine your *behavior*, and your behavior will determine how you *feel* about yourself.

Let me give you an example of what I mean. The *truth* of God's word in 1 Peter 2:9 says, **"I am a chosen race, a royal Priesthood."** I now *believe* that I am a Queen to the King of Kings. I choose to *behave* as royalty like Proverbs 31:10 says, **"A wife of noble character, who can find? Her value is far greater than rubies."** You see I am not out looking for a husband anymore, or looking for love in all the wrong places. I no longer go out on useless dates just so I can feel better about myself or to feel more like a woman. Nor am I dating just so I can have something to do on a Saturday night, or to get some free food. Ouch! I know that one hurt.

The truth is that I have a husband who is so much more than that. God's word says in Isaiah 54:5, **"Your husband is your maker. The Lord Almighty is his name."** Now, I am committed to being the best Bride of Christ, woman and mother that I can be. That my dear single mom is all you will ever need to be happy in life.

As a single mom, you have to understand and accept what Colossians 2:10 says, **"In Him you have been made complete."** If God has an earthly husband for you he will be looking for a woman who knows who she really is "In Christ," and acts like it too!

My dear single mom, when you start to understand and live out these scriptures so will your children. I read these scriptures to my son Eric every day, so he will know who he is in Christ. Our children need to hear sound and positive things from their mother. With all they are bombarded with from school, television and radio they need to know they are accepted, secure and significant in God's eyes and their mother's.

My son has memorized these verses for himself. Our children need to get truth engrained in their mind just like we do. They must learn how to win the battle for their minds on their own. The last thing I need is for my child to grow up wearing the false titles the world has to offer him. I refuse to let my son live a defeated life.

I want to share a story with you how the word of God changed my son's thinking. When Eric was only eight years old, he came home from school with a hurt look on his face. When I asked him what was wrong, he said someone on the bus called him stupid. I asked him if it was true, and he said, "No". Then I asked him to tell me who he was. He recited off those scriptures, and when he was done an enormous smile came on his face. He went out to play basketball and acted like nothing bad had ever happened.

There are so many voices shouting for our attention. We have to decide which voice we are going to listen to. Will it be our own voice? What other people say? Or the enemy whispering lies in our ear? The best choice is to do what Matthew 17:5 says, **"This is my son, listen to Him."**

So how did I answer Dr. Stanley's question? I just said I was a child of God disguised here on earth as a speaker and author.

Questions:
1. What are the false label's you are wearing?
2. Identify who gave them to you.
3. What will you do with the false labels?
4. What will you say the next time someone asks you about who you are?
5. Read the scriptures out loud to yourself and to your children on a daily basis.

Note: "Victory Over the Darkness," Neil Anderson

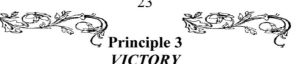

Principle 3
VICTORY

"Now in a large house there are not only gold and sliver vessels, but also vessels of wood and of earthen ware, and some to honor and some to dishonor. Therefore, if anyone cleanses himself from these things, he will be a vessel for honor, sanctified, useful to the Master, prepared for every good work."
2 Timothy 2:20-21

These last few years of single motherhood have undoubtedly been the greatest experience of my life. I feel whole and complete in God alone, and there is nothing missing in my life now. My wounds and hurts from the past have been healed, and I am experiencing real love from Jesus Christ and other people like I have never known. I am also completely satisfied with my single mom life. For the first time I feel terrific about my self from the inside out. My life is filled with purpose and meaning, focus and order and balance and harmony. Tremendous joy and peace fill each day of my life. God is cradling me in his arms, He is holding and protecting me, and I am resting fully in Him. My eyes have been opened to a new way of life. It seems as if a black veil was lifted off of them. I see my position with God clearly now, and from an entirely different point of view. I am living from the love of God instead of my own mind, will and emotions. Life as a single mom is good. It is really, really good.

How did I ever get to this incredible point in my life? I did what Paul said to do in Ephesians 4:31, **"Get rid of all bitterness, rage, anger, brawling and slander, along with every form of malice.** As a new single mom I felt angry, rejected and full of fear and anxiety. I harbored hatred against certain people; especially my ex-husband. Inside I was bound up in emotional darkness, and a prisoner to internal rage and fury. I did a remarkable job of fooling everyone, including myself, to believe that I could handle all of this on my own. I also lied to everyone and told them that everything was just fine.

My Pastor preached a message one Sunday on "Strongholds" that changed my life forever. I was so overwhelmed by what I just heard I could not move when service was over. I sat in my chair with tears streaming down my face saying, "I just never knew." What I learned that day about strongholds is that they are Satan's way of controlling you from things that have happened in your past. They keep you from fully understanding the truth about God's love and acceptance of you.

Once we accept Jesus as our Lord and Savior the bright powerful light of His truth shines into our heart. This is what turn's the darkness of sin into a bright light of forgiving love. The penetrating power of the Holy Spirit is what comes into your heart and changes you. God's love can not fully penetrate your heart if Satan still has a grip on you from the past.

Satan causes *blockage* and acts as a *filter* to what you can receive from God's truth. It is just like going to the beach. You put on sunscreen to protect your skin from burning, and sunglasses to shade the sunlight from your eyes. The SPF in the sunscreen acts as a filter and blocks certain rays from penetrating your skin. The sunglasses act as a shade over your eyes that keep you from seeing the true light of the sun. The sunscreen and sunglasses act in the same way as strongholds do; they filter, shade and block God's love and the healing rays of His truth.

I learned from my Pastor's message how so many things from our past, starting at conception with the main focus on our younger years of puberty affect the way we think and act today. Situations from you possibly being an unwanted pregnancy, if you were born the wrong sex that a parent wanted, being adopted, a tragic event that occurred in your youth; maybe the death of a parent or loved one, a violation; perhaps you may have been sexually abused or raped, harsh words spoken from parents, parental neglect, involvement in the occult, exposure to pornography, transference from past generations and past sex partners, perhaps your parents divorced or you have experienced one yourself, and our own willful disobedience all cause strongholds in our lives.

As I sat alone that night thinking about the sermon, I recalled some memories from my own childhood. I faced some truly painful things when I was young. Unfortunately, this is real life and these things happen with people. A lot of the destructive behavior we face from other people comes from strongholds passed down from generation to generation. These things must be dealt with and broken in our lives, and in our children.

I sat at my kitchen table with my head in my hands saying, "No wonder I am the way that I am. No wonder I feel such bitterness, rejection, fear, insecurity and have no self worth. No wonder I can never feel good about the way I look. No wonder I never felt like a soft woman or why I thought sex was what love is all about." I could never understand why I just could not say a sincere, "Thank you" when someone paid me a compliment. I always had to find a way to put myself down to them.

I learned that Satan attacks the soul; the precise place that controls our mind (how we think), our will (how we choose) and our emotions (how we feel). The soul is the part of us that houses our deepest hurts and feelings. Satan uses strongholds of deceit, rejection, control, fear and insecurity, bitterness, confusion, pride, independence, jealousy, heaviness and sexual impurity to cause you to remember an event or moment from your past. Then he lodges that event in you like a hook, and controls you like a puppet on a string to think and do things that are not of God. Strongholds also prevent us from giving and receiving love, understanding and acceptance in other relationships.

With a better understanding about strongholds, I finally realized why I was not able to accept God's truth about me. I just love what Proverbs 31:10 says, **"A wife of noble character who can find, her value is far greater than rubies."** I also love 1 Peter 2:9 that says, **"You are a chosen people, a royal priesthood."** As beautiful as those words are to me I could never think of my self as noble, valuable, better than rubies or royalty. I never imagined that I was worthy of or deserved something as beautiful as that.

The more I learned about strongholds I recognized the control Satan had over my life. I accepted the horrible names I was called in my childhood as truth. I thought that I was fat, ugly and never worthy of a handsome godly man for a husband. I genuinely thought that no one good looking would ever look at me. I never finished college, so I viewed myself as someone not worthy of a husband that was a successful business executive. I thought, "What good would I be to him not fully educated and fat?" I started to realize how unhealthy I truly was.

I kept wondering though if the power of Satan was destroyed at the cross why am I not living in that victory? I felt the Holy Spirit say, *"Look at the way you view yourself. It is blocked and shaded from the truth, and you are deceived. You do not feel worthy. You do not feel pretty. You do not feel that anyone recognizes what you do. You do not feel valuable. You do not feel loved and accepted. Stop living off of your feelings and live off of my*

truth." That was it! I was not living off of the power of
the Holy Spirit and God's word. I was living from my soul
and letting Satan control me like a puppet on a string. I
was deceived, and that is why "I just never knew." Just
then the verse from John 8:31 came to my mind that says,
**"You shall know the truth and the truth shall set you
free."**

I wanted to live a life of truth and stop living from lies. I
recalled the verse from Psalms 2:3 that says, **"Let us break
their chains and throw off of their fetters."** The last
sentence from my favorite verse also came to my mind
from Jeremiah 29:11-14 that says, **"You will seek me and
find me when you seek me with all of your heart. I will
be found by you, and will bring you back from
captivity."** I realized that I was living in captivity, and I
wanted out!

I thought about the story in John 5:6-9 that says, **"An
invalid man had tried to get into the healing pool when
the angel stirred it for thirty-eight years. When Jesus
saw him lying there and learned that he had been in this
condition for a long time he asked him, "Do you want to
get well?" "Sir, the invalid replied, "I have no one to
help me into the pool when the water is stirred. While I
am trying to get in, someone else goes down ahead of
me." Then Jesus said to him, "Get up, take up your
mat and walk." At once the man was cured; he picked
up his mat and he walked."**

I felt the Holy Spirit say, *"Do you want to get well?"* I
did not know that I was sick until I heard about
strongholds. It was at that *pivotal* moment that I knew I
wanted to be healed. I wanted to be whole, complete and
healthy in Christ. I wanted it for myself and my son. I was
willing to do whatever it took so my son did not grow up in
the turmoil of bondage. If I was going to experience the

complete love of God, I had to give Satan an eviction notice from my life. Like the invalid man trying to get to the healing pool I needed to rise. I had to experience the power of the cross and stop letting Satan control and manipulate me. I needed to take my mat and roll it up. I had to put my past in perspective and start doing what healthy people do. They walk in victory from the truth of God's word. I realized that no one could do this for me. This was something only the power of the Holy Spirit working in me could do. All I had to do was start offering myself to God. If I would start walking, He would start healing me.

I wanted to experience the love of Christ, so I did it. I "Got up" the next day and made an appointment with my Pastor and Woman's Ministry Leader. I "Picked up my mat" and journeyed into my past with them. This was the hardest task I have ever done in my life. I confessed all of my known sins and asked God to forgive me. I also chose to forgive everyone that ever hurt me. I cried for hours and it was radical heart surgery. When we were done I was cured. Instantly the pain that once gripped my heart was replaced with God's love and forgiveness.

I remember the first words I spoke after the tears stopped flowing. It was the most incredible thing that I have ever said about myself. As I spoke the words, "I feel so beautiful" I knew I was going on a journey of a lifetime with God. Darkness was in the past, and I saw true light for the first time in my life. Finally I was able to see myself as God sees me. Psalms 139:13-14 says, **"For you know my innermost being; you knit me together in my mother's womb. I praise you because I am fearfully and wonderfully made; your works are beautiful, I know that full well."** When I look at myself I see a piece of art, a true masterpiece made by my creator's hands.

The horrible memories from my past were wiped away as Romans 8:1 says, **"Therefore, there is now no condemnation for those who are in Christ Jesus."** Now that my eyes are open to truth I can live in the victory of the cross. I understand that Jesus did not die on the cross for me to live a defeated and depressed life in bondage to the enemy. God wants us to be victorious, and Jesus rose from the dead to enforce that victory in us. I also knew this was going to be a battle with Satan for the rest of my life. He could not possibly be thrilled with what God just did for me. I had just declared war on Satan, and I needed to learn how to fight.

We live in victory as single moms by understanding our position with Jesus. Paul says in Ephesians 1:1 that we are to be faithful "In Christ." As women of God, we are exalted and enthroned above all principalities and powers. Ephesians 2:6 says, **"God raised us up with Christ and seated us with him in the heavenly realms in Christ Jesus."** The heavenly places are where Christ is presently enthroned. Ephesians 1:20-22 says, **"He raised him from the dead and seated him at his right hand in the heavenly realms, far above all rule and authority, power and dominion, and every title that can be given, not only in the present age but also in the one to come. And God placed all things under his feet and appointed him to be head over everything for the church."**

When we understand our position in Christ, we believe that everything under His feet is under ours also as believers. We are ambassadors of heaven and here on earth we have the authority of Jesus. Our battle with Satan takes charge in the heavenly realm. It is already won before it even starts. Ephesians 6:12 says, **"For our struggle is not against flesh and blood, but against the rulers, against the authorities, against the powers of this dark world**

and against the spiritual forces of evil in the heavenly realms." As believers we do not belong to Satan nor do our children. Satan has no authority over us for we are God's property. All the kingdoms of this world are overthrown, and Satan is defeated.

I finally understood this point one day at the pool when my son wanted to race. I laughed to myself when he said he could beat me. This five year old boy was fully convinced that he could beat his mom who used to be a competitive swimmer. In Eric's mind he did not know that he would lose. From my perspective, he was already defeated before we even started the race. That is exactly how we must perceive spiritual warfare.

It is easy at times to say to Satan, "In the name of Jesus, shut up and go away." James 4:7 says, **"Submit to God, resist the devil and he will flee from you."** Other times it will take prayer, and sometimes fasting to win the battle. It is not that I do not take Satan seriously. He is dangerous as John 10:10 says, **"The enemy comes to steal, kill and destroy."** I have learned not to fear Satan anymore. I realize how much time I wasted paralyzed and living in bondage. How could you be afraid of Satan when you are sitting in heavenly places? The battle with Satan is not a power encounter; it is a truth encounter. The Holy Spirit and Satan cannot exist in the same place. Satan is the Father of lies and Jesus is the way, the truth and the life. It is simply a matter of lies verses truth. If it is not in the Bible then it is not true. That is why my dear single mom you must be in the Bible every day to win this battle. It is your shield, your protection and your victory for you and your children.

On this earth the temptation to sin is enormous and Satan will relentlessly attack to draw us back to him. It is essential as a single mom to make a daily decision to live in victory. It is not easy for me, and it is a minute-by-minute commitment to live a victorious life. If I allow sin, temptation, wrong attitudes, wrong words and past hurts to go unconfessed, unchallenged or unchanged I leave the door wide open with a welcome mat out for Satan. Victory comes when I choose to stay focused on Christ and not the difficult circumstances of single motherhood.

You cannot win this spiritual war on your own. It takes heavenly weapons which are the word of God, and spiritual armor. Ephesians 6:13-18 says, **"Therefore, put on the full armor of God, so that when the day of evil comes, you may be able to stand your ground, and after you have done everything, stand. Stand firm then with the belt of truth buckled around your waist, with the breastplate of righteousness in place, and with your feet fitted with the readiness that comes from the gospel of peace. In addition to all of this, take up the shield of faith, with which you can extinguish all the flaming arrows of the evil one. Take the helmet of salvation and the sword of the spirit, which is the word of God. And pray in the Spirit on all occasions with all kinds of prayers and requests."**

As single moms, we must be strong in the Lord to protect our children and ourselves. The Lord is willing to do His part, and we must do ours to ensure victory for the day. You would not go to work nor have your children go to school without any clothes on, now would you? Do not leave the house without getting spiritually dressed, so you are not entirely defenseless to Satan's schemes. Put on God's armor piece by piece and declare his promises for you today.

My son is now living in victory and experiencing the love and joy of Christ. When I came home from my meeting with my Pastor, my son took one look at me and said, "Mommy, you look so happy, what happened to you?" I told him all about it and to this day the greatest moment for me as a mother was when my son put his little hand in mine and led me to our prayer chair and asked me to pray with him. Strongholds came off of him when he forgave his dad for leaving our family. I prayed over generational strongholds that were in me, and his father that have been passed down to him, and in the name of Jesus broke those strongholds in his life. He has gone a step further and broken those strongholds over himself when he was just nine years old. He is such a healthy young man now spiritually, emotionally, mentally and physically. Life as a single mom is good. It is really, really good!

My prayer is that you too will rise, and pick up your mat to do what healthy single moms do. They walk in victory and raise healthy children that walk in victory also.

Go through Section Two of the downloadable Workbook. To access the Workbook, send an email to: bookresources@hope4singlemoms.com

Note: "Demolishing Strongholds, Mike and Sue Dowgiewicz";
"Vanquishing the Enemy," Ron Phillips

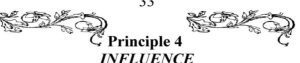

Principle 4
INFLUENCE

"These words, which I am commanding you today, shall be on your heart. You shall teach them diligently to your sons and shall talk to them when you sit in your house and when you walk by the way and when you lie down and when you rise up. You shall bind them as a sign on your hand and they shall be as frontals on your forehead."
Deuteronomy 6:6-9

    The first thought that raced through my mind as a new single mom was, "What is going to happen to my son without a father in the house? How is he going to become a man from being raised only by his mother?"

    The head of the house is not what God designed for us to be. As a woman, this new position felt extremely unnatural and overwhelming. I was not trained for this role, or in any way prepared for it. All I knew to do was fall on my knees and ask God for help. I needed to know my son was going to be alright without a father. The Lord graciously answered my prayer in two different ways.

    The first answer was from the Bible in 2 Timothy 1:5 that says, **"For I am mindful of the sincere faith within you, which first dwelt in your grandmother Lois and your mother Eunice, and I am sure that it is in you as well."** This was an extraordinarily encouraging verse for me as a new single mom. Notice that Timothy's father is not mentioned in this verse. Look at what these two women did in the life of young Timothy without the help of a Christian father. They poured their faith into him, and when he grew up he became the beloved son of the apostle Paul; the greatest apostle that ever lived. This verse taught me to put the word of God into myself and then into my son. I knew if I did my part, God would do His. I trusted that He would bring "Paul's" into my son's life to mentor him into adult hood. By the grace of God I saw the fruit of my labor when my son was only ten years old. God brought some awesome Christian men into Eric's life, and still continues to do so.

The second answer to my prayer was an article I read about Anne Graham Lotz, the daughter of Billy Graham. Now you might be thinking, "How can her story relate to me as a single mom?" She was not raised by a single mom and she has Billy Graham for a father. Billy Graham traveled ten months out of the year. This meant his wife Ruth was in charge of raising her family practically on her own. Anne said what influenced her life the most was seeing her mother reading the Bible. If Anne woke up in the middle of the night, or early in the morning, she found her mom in God's word.

Now, Ruth Graham's children are leading voices for the Gospel all around the world. I believe God has an extraordinary plan for our children also. It starts by what we do right now in the position we are in as single moms.

The highest calling we have as single mothers is being the Spiritual Leader of our home. I followed the example of these great mothers by getting the word of God into me, and into my son. I set my alarm to wake up earlier, so I could read my Bible in the peaceful still quiet of the early morning. When my son got up, he saw my open Bible on the kitchen table. He started his day assured that his mom was in God's word before doing anything else that morning. (With the exception of making strong coffee of course.) While Eric and I ate breakfast, I read a Proverb to him. Can you believe that to this day my son, at the age of fifteen, still enjoys reading the Proverbs out loud in the morning together? I took my Bible with me every where I went and continued my study through out the day. I read my Bible in the car at stop lights and in traffic jams. I also read during my lunch hour at work. When I came home from work, I read the Bible to Eric at the dinner table, and before he went to bed. After Eric went to bed, I read and studied my Bible some more.

Sure enough, Eric would wake up from a dream and come out of his room to find me. What would he find me doing? Reading my Bible. Time after time, my son saw his mom reading God's word.

Because of all the mistakes I made, one of the many blessings of reading the Bible is that my son feels safe now. He knows I try to learn as much as I can about the Bible, and then try to live by it. God's word brings immense comfort and peace to us, especially in the madness of this cruel, crazy, mixed up world.

Before I decided to spend my extra time in the Bible, my son saw me depressed, crying my eyes out or gossiping on the phone. Other times he would see me lying on the couch watching pointless TV and stuffing my mouth with junk food. He also saw other things that I do not want to mention. All of these activities were extremely unhealthy. I brought myself down and my whole house with me. What influence would any unhealthy activity you may be involved with have on your children's lives?

The key to Spiritual Leadership is to look at God's word for the answer to every question, and teach your children to do the same. When Eric has a question, or if he is dealing with a problem I just say, "Let's see what God says about that." Letting God's word lead takes a load off of our shoulders as single mothers. It lets God do the parenting for us. You do not have to be weighed down with making all of the decisions on your own. Your job is to enforce God's word. This way the children will see that you are not making up the rules as you go along. You are simply following Divine Principles already established by God.

It is funny how most children will think that maybe they should at least listen to what God has to say. Children trust adults, and look to us for guidance and advice. It is through their relationship with us that they learn to know and trust God.

In the Principle of Hope, we learned the way we tend to perceive what God is like comes from the way important people in our life have failed us or mistreated us. As single mothers, we must draw our children close to God in everything we do. This will help them see that God is a good God, and they can trust Him.

Recently Eric wanted to go to his freshman dance. He had his eye on a young lady and asked me if he could take her. After praying about it, I did not feel she was the right girl for him, even though I never met her. I asked my mentors to pray about it also, and they felt the same way I did. Eric still asked her, and the whole episode blew up in his face. In the end, they did not go to the dance.

After he had some time to think about things, he realized he wanted to take her for all the wrong reasons. He also discovered that she was not the girl that he thought she was after all. Eric admitted that he should have known better if after praying, both my mentors and I thought it was wrong. He realized that it was God that said no, and that it was for his own safety. God knew that girl was not the right one for him to be with, and Eric finally realized it too. He was able to see that God is a good God from this situation, and that he could trust Him. Eric also said that he trusted me with the direction for his life because he knows I do not make decisions on my own. I go to God for the answer.

What does it take to be the Spiritual Leader of your home? First you must be saved. You must have Christ in your life and accepted Him as your Lord and Savior.

Second, you must be in Divine Alignment which means to put our spirit, soul and body all under the blood covering of Jesus. Galatians 5:16 says, **"Walk in the Spirit, and you shall not fulfill the lust of the flesh."** When we walk in the Spirit, we hear God's voice, avoid sin, receive guidance for our life and experience daily peace. When guided by His Spirit, we walk in His power and authority, and we are spiritually protected.

In the Principle of Victory, we talked about the soul which is our mind, will and emotions. The soul houses our disappointments, hurts, anger, depression and memories. It needs spiritual protection to heal and be restored from the past. This allows you to mature in your Christian walk.

Third, you must belong to a church, for this identifies you as a believer. We were made for relationships, and you need fellowship with other believers. The church is also where you're God- given gifts and talents are best utilized. The church mobilizes us as a believer to be sent out into the world, and educates us about God.

You do not have to be a bible scholar to be the Spiritual Leader of your home. You just need a willing spirit, and a Bible that you can easily read and understand. Visit your local Christian book store and look over some Bibles to see which one is right for you. The point is to just get started.

While reading Rick Warrens book, "The Purpose Driven Life" I came to the page where he asked Bill Bright, the founder of Campus Crusade for Christ, why God used and blessed him so much. Bill said that as a young man he made a contract with God where he wrote, "From this day forward I am a slave of Jesus Christ." I wanted to be used by God in an enormous way too so, I wrote the same contract in my book. When Eric read my copy of the book, he was extremely moved by what I wrote. He asked me for a pen and wrote the same contract out for himself. Now, he is highly involved with me at Hope & Help for the Single

Mom. He even travels and speaks with me at conferences all around the country. Eric also just agreed to author the "21Principles for Kids." I truly believe that God will use Eric in a powerful way to be a voice for Him all around the world.

I tried my best to model the two women at the beginning of this Principle. I read the word of God for myself, and then poured God's word into Eric. I also taught him the importance of daily prayer and reading God's word.   I knew if I did my part, God would do His. You can have the same influence in your home as well. It is never too early or too late to get started.

1. **Have you accepted the responsibility of being the Spiritual Leader of your home?**
2. **What changes do you need to make to be the Spiritual Leader?**
3. **What areas of your life may not be a good example to your children?**
4. **What changes do you need to make to have those areas line up with God's will?**
5. **Are you in Divine Alignment? Can you hear God's voice? Does your life style offer you Spiritual Protection? Are you growing and maturing as a Christian?**
6. **If you answered no to any questions in #5, what changes do you need to make?**

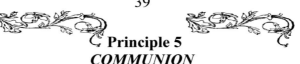

Principle 5
COMMUNION

"And in the morning, rising up a great while before the day, he went out, and departed into a solitary place, and there he prayed."
Mark 1:35

Prayer is our communication with God, and it must be a vital part of our daily Christian life. The Principle of Communion is designed to teach you how to pray as Jesus taught his disciples in Matthew 6:9-15, **"Pray then this way: Our Father who is in heaven, Hallowed be your name. Your kingdom come, your will be done, on earth as it is in heaven. Give us this day our daily bread. And forgive us our debts, as we also have forgiven our debtors. And do not lead us into temptation, but deliver us from evil. For Yours is the kingdom and the power and the glory forever. Amen."**

This is often called the Lord's Prayer because Jesus taught it to his disciples. We can use it as a model for our own prayers too. My goal in this Principle is to share with you how I pray in the morning and start my day with the Lord.

I like to start my prayer time with some praise and worship music first, and then I read from the book of Psalms. This sets my heart and spirit with praise to our Father, and brings me closer to Him. I start my prayer time on my knees, and then I often get up and walk around while praying. My mind can start to wander and this helps keep me focused. Some days I have to follow this outline word for word and read it out loud to keep my mind from straying. The enemy hates it when you pray and he will do anything he can to distract you and get your mind off course from praying. Below is my outline for prayer. Please feel free to use this word by word if you have to in order to keep your mind focused.

Our Father who art in heaven, Hallowed by your name.
Thank you Father that I can call you Abba Father and
Daddy. Thank you that you are my **Jehovah-Tsidkenu**;
my righteousness. Thank you that I am righteous and
forgiven because of the blood of Jesus. Thank you that you
are my **Jehovah-M'kaddesh**; my sanctifier. Thank you
that you set me apart for your service. I choose to be
different from this world and follow your word. Thank you
that you are my **Jehovah -Rophe**; my healer. Thank you
that by the stripes you took on your back I am healed
spiritually, emotionally, mentally, physically, socially and
financially. Thank you that you are my **Jehovah -Jireh**; my
provider. Thank you that you have made provisions for my
sins here on earth through your son Jesus, and that you
provide everything that I need here on earth according to
your riches and glory. Thank you that you are my **Jehovah-
Shammah**; your presence is everywhere. Thank you that
you will never leave me nor forsake me. Thank you that
you are my **Jehovah-Shalom**; my peace. Father it's your
peace that surpasses all understanding that allows me to be
content and satisfied in every situation. Thank you that you
are my **Jehovah-Rhoi;** my shepherd, my companion and
my friend. Thank you that you lead me, guide me and care
for me like no one else can. Thank you for your voice
behind me that says, "This is the way, walk in it." Thank
you that you are my **Jehovah-Nissi**; my banner, my
victory. Thank you that Jesus goes in battle before us and
gives us the victory that makes us more than conquerors.
    Father you are the vine and I am the branch. I am
nothing with out you, I can do nothing with out you, I can
have nothing with out you and I am lost without you. I ask

you to take this dead branch and graft it to your true living vine. Holy Spirit I invite into my life today; come Holy Spirit come. I ask you to drain me of me from the top of my head out through the souls of my feet, and fill me with all of you. Father you must increase and I must decrease.

Today I choose to be a spiritual woman of God, and I desire to walk all the days of my life in the Spirit. Body in the name of Jesus, I command you to submit to my soul. Soul in the name of Jesus, I command you to submit to my Spirit. Soul you will not take over the headship of my life. I will not be manipulated by the pain, rejection and fear that are a part of you. Spirit in the name of Jesus, I command you to submit to the Holy Spirit of the great, mighty Jehovah God. I choose to receive no help, strength or guidance from any other spirit other than the Holy Spirit.

Blood of Jesus cover my home from the top of the roof to the bottom of the foundation, from the front to the back to the left to the right.   Post your holy warring angels around my property and let no weapon formed against it, myself, my son, my dogs, my ministry, business or possessions prosper or succeed in the name of Jesus.

Thank you that through your son Jesus I am well, blessed and highly favored. Bless me Oh Lord indeed, enlarge my territory, have your hand with me and keep evil far away from me that I may cause no harm to anyone. I pray for a pure heart and clean hands that will put me in the position to receive your blessings today. Don't let me miss out on one of them today. I am expecting today to be the greatest day of my life. Today I declare that I have the favor of God. Thank you Father that your favor surrounds me like a shield. Thank you Father that because I am a child of the most high God, you want to assist me, provide special advantages to me and for me to receive preferential treatment. Thank you that your favor is opening doors for me that no man can shut. It is your favor that is causing me to be at the right place at the right time today. It is your favor that is bringing wonderful opportunities my way today. Father your word says that wealth and riches are in your house and your righteousness endures for ever. I speak from Psalm 118, **"Do send prosperity today."** Thank you Father that through you everything I touch prospers and succeeds. Thank you that I am a lender and not a borrower. Thank you that you have my best interests at heart and you are working out everything to my good. Thank you that through you I am well equipped and able to do what you have called me to do today. Thank you that I am a victor and not a victim. It is your favor that is causing my Eric to be great and mighty for you around the world; use him in a big way. Your favor is causing churches and people to minister to single mothers through the 21Principles. Father your favor is helping me reach every single mother every where in the world for your glory. (Declare your God given favor over every area of your life. Call out your God ordained blessings according to His word.)

Thy Kingdom come, Thy will be done.

Father I pray, "Thy Kingdom Come, Thy will be done" over my life today. Not my will but your will, not my plan but your plan. I have plan B, and you have Plan A. I invite you to rearrange my plans for your divine perfect plan and will to be done in my life today. I pray that you establish your Kingdom in me; righteousness, joy and peace. I give you control over my heart, my mind, my soul, my will, my emotions and body today. I refuse to tolerate Satan or let him thwart your awesome plan for me today. I pray for your divine wisdom and discernment in everything I will be involved in today." Next, I talk to God about every detail of my day. I have my prayer list of things I need God to take care of for me, and my journal to write down what I hear from God. It is such a thrill to watch God work by crossing a line through the prayers that He answers, and wait in expectancy for Him to answer the rest.

The next step I take is to pray for my son. I pray, "Thy Kingdom Come Thy will be done over Eric today." (Pray for each one of your children specifically.) Father not my will but Your will for Eric's life today. Father I pray that you bless him with wisdom and discernment beyond his years. Bless him Oh Lord indeed; enlarge his territory, have your hand with him and keep evil far away from him that he may cause no harm to anyone. I pray that Eric would be a godly friend to others and that you bring good, godly friends into his life. Take out anyone in his life that does not belong there, and replace them with ones that you have chosen for him. Father I ask you for favor with all of his teachers and coaches today. Help Eric to be all that you have ordained for him to be, and use all the intelligence that you already have blessed him with. I declare your favor over a full ride basketball scholarship to UNC Chapel Hill and that he would live out his dream to play for Roy Williams as a Tar Heel. (I stand in the gap for him praying big and into the future). Father, in the name of Jesus I declare that Eric is well, blessed and highly favored and that everything he touches prospers and succeeds. Your favor is bringing wonderful financial opportunities his way. Bless his pet sitting service in abundance Father. It is your favor that is bringing the right clients at the right time to him. Thank you that Eric is a lender and not a borrower. In the name of Jesus I say no to Eric ever drinking, smoking, doing drugs, chemicals, alcohol or putting anything else harmful into his body. I say no to accidents, illnesses, injuries, rape, sexual molestation or predators of any kind; keep them away from my son. Father I pray that Eric will walk the straight and narrow path and not ever turn to the right or to the left. I

declare in the name of Jesus that Eric will be a virgin until
the day he marries and that his first kiss will be at the alter
when the Pastor says, "You may kiss your Bride." I pray
that Eric's wife will be a virgin until the day she marries
Eric. I pray that her first kiss will also be on her wedding
day to Eric. Lord, make her a virtuous woman and give her
a heart for missions. I plead the blood of Jesus over my son
and wrap a hedge of protection around him from the top of
his head to the soles of his feet, from the front to the back
to the left to the right. Let no weapon formed against him
prosper or succeed. I stand in the gap for him and put on
the armor of God; his buckle of truth, breastplate of
righteousness, footprints of peace, helmet of salvation,
shield of faith and I pray he uses the sword of your Spirit.

Then I pray like this over his future wife, and my
immediate family members. Another resource that I use for
Eric is a book called, "The Power of a Praying Parent" by
Stormie Omartian. I read the prayer that matches the day of
the month over him every night.

Then I pray for my Pastor, his family, our church and our
nation and leaders.

Father, I lift up my Pastor to you. (Insert your Pastors
name) Thank you for his shepherd's heart Lord. Bless him
with wisdom and revelation as he prays and studies your
word. Keep his family safe. I pray for the other Pastors
and Elders of my church. (Call them out by name) Anoint
them, speak to them and direct them. Bless them with
wisdom and strength to fulfill the vision you have given
Pastor for our church.

I pray over the leadership of our church. (Speak out their
names) Show us how to breathe in through fellowship and
breathe out in evangelism. I pray over our congregation
that the people of our church will be faithful to you Lord,

their families and to the vision that God has given Pastor for our church.

I pray over the harvest; the North, South, East and West and declare today there are souls that need to be released into the Kingdom of God and our church. I command you in the name of Jesus to release every person who is supposed to become a part of God's Kingdom and our church body today. (I stand facing each direction and declare this.) Father, bless our President with the wisdom of God, that spiritual leaders will walk and govern by God's word, be people of prayer, and be kept by the power of God. I pray over our city, state and national leaders. (Name the city, state and leaders)

Father, I pray that I am in your perfect will; that I spend time daily with you in your word and prayer, that I am in fellowship with my church, that I have diligent, balanced work habits, and that I obey in giving financially.

Give us this day our daily bread

Father, give us this day our daily bread and thank you that you provide our daily needs. (Pray over your needs and pray specifically and in detail for what you need) I will persevere in asking these things until the answer comes!

Forgive us our debts, as we also have forgiven our debtors.

Father, I ask you to forgive me of my sins. (Confess your sins to God) Show me Lord anything that I am letting into my life that is not of you. Help me hate my sin with a perfect hatred and deliver me from it. I choose to forgive others that have hurt me and not keep bitterness in my heart. I will love those who hurt me, bless those who curse me and do good to those who hate me.

I pray that the fruit of the Holy Spirit be greater than ever in me.   Fill me with more love, joy, peace, patience, kindness, goodness, faithfulness, gentleness and self control.

And do not lead us into temptation, but deliver us from evil.

Wrap a hedge of protection around me from the crown of my head to the soles of my feet, from the front to the back to the left to the right.

I put on my armor today.   I put on my:

Buckle of Truth: Jesus, you are the way, the truth and the life.

Breast plate of Righteousness: I am whole and complete in you Lord. The only person I am is the one that God says I am.

Footprints of Peace: I will stand firm in the truth of God in the storms of life.   I can do all things through Christ who strengthens me.

Helmet of Salvation: I know that I have the mind of Christ.   I have not been given a spirit of fear, but of power love and a sound mind.

Shield of Faith: I am protected from all that Satan throws at me.   I rebuke temptations, accusations, distractions, depression, fear, worry, anxiety. I put my trust in you Lord and declare; "I have been crucified with Christ; yet it is not I that live but Christ that lives within me.   This life I live I live by faith."

Sword of the Spirit: The word of God is truth and is used to attack Satan. The word of God is a living sword. It is penetrating and powerful. The sharp sword of the Word of God exposes the enemy's lies.

 For Yours is the kingdom, power and the glory now and forever. AMEN!

What plan can you implement into your life for a deeper, more intimate prayer life?

Notes: "Could You Not Tarry One Hour?" Dr. Larry Lea; "Your Best Life Now," Joel Osteen.

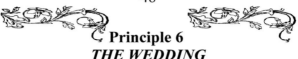

Principle 6
THE WEDDING

"Your maker is your husband; The Lord Almighty is His name."
Isaiah 54:5

"OK Lord, I am ready for that Godly husband now," I said to the Lord early one Saturday morning. I was sitting at my kitchen table in my very "comfortable" sweat suit (comfortable is a polite name for extremely nasty, old and worn out) crying over how lonely I was. The Lord said back to me, *"Lori, what in the world would I do that to my man of God for? Look at you, you are a mess. You need to learn to be my Bride first."*

"Well" I said back to the Lord in a rage. "I do not like what you are saying, and I do not ever recall reading in the Bible that I am a mess." The Lord spoke to my spirit again and said, *"Read Psalms 40 in The Message."* I quickly went through my stack of Bibles and found The Message. I opened it to Psalms 40 and breezed through the passage. My heart suddenly skipped as I came to the end of the psalm. There it was just as God said, **"And me? I'm a mess. I'm nothing and have nothing; make something of me. You can do it; you've got what it takes- but God, don't put it off."**

I felt terrible about what God saw that morning. If he has seen that "comfortable" sweat suit once, he has seen it a thousand times. It is all I wore around the house for the last year. I still had makeup on, and dried up mascara under my eyes. I was constantly exhausted, so I stopped taking care of myself properly. All I could think was, "Who cares? There's no one here to look good for anyhow."

As I felt the Lord look past me, I knew he saw the dishes still sitting in the sink from several days ago. My house was anything but tidy, and God did not need sand to write anything in as He did in the Bible. The dust was thick enough for that. The laundry was not done, and he did not need to open my refrigerator to see that it was completely empty. I had not gone grocery shopping, and there was no meal plan for the week to make a grocery list for. The meals seemed to be haphazard. I either threw something together for Eric, or we wasted money and went out to eat.

I recalled how obsessed I had become lately about desiring a husband. It seemed that if a man paid the least bit of attention to me I would say, "Is that him Lord, is that my husband?" My constant prayer to God was, "When Lord. When is my husband going to come?"

After reading Psalm 40, I started to understand what the Lord was trying to tell me. This scene is not what a man of God would look for in a wife. Suddenly one of my favorite verses came to mind from Proverbs 31:10 that says, **"A wife of noble character who can find? Her value is far greater than rubies."** I was confused by what God meant to be His bride first. How do you have an intimate relationship with Christ?

When I first heard the phrase, "Intimacy with Christ" I had a sick sexual experience in my mind. I had a faulty definition of what true love, passion and intimacy actually meant. As single mothers, we need time alone with God to learn what unconditional, non physical love truly is. In other words, *we need to experience intimacy without a physical touch.*

I felt like God was asking me to stop dating and spend a year alone with Him. I panicked at the plan and said to him, "You mean be all alone with you for a year God? If there is no man in my life I will be terribly lonely. Who will validate me and make me feel like I am worth something? Who will I have to look good for? Who will take me out? How will there be any meaning in my life if I am all alone with just you?" The Lord said, *"I will do all of that for you. I want to show you what a perfect husband will look like, and how that will make you feel. I want you to understand that you are my Queen, and I want to treat you like one. You will never know what a godly husband will look like for yourself, or what a godly father will look like for Eric until you learn what true love is from me first."*

I started to think about the men that I allowed into my life, and I have to admit I did not make wise choices. I never thought that I was worthy of a Godly man, or that one would ever want me. I settled for anyone that would even look at me.

I thought of the verse in 2 Timothy 3:2-7 that says, **"People will be lovers of themselves, lovers of money, boastful, proud, abusive, disobedient to their parents, ungrateful, unholy, without love, unforgiving, slanderous, without self-control, brutal, not lovers of the good, treacherous, rash, conceited, lovers of pleasure rather than lovers of God – having a form of godliness but denying its power. Have nothing to do with them. They are the kind who worm their way into homes and gain control over weak willed women."** Why do you think we allow that class of men into our life? Now you might be thinking, "Oh good, in this Principle we get to bash these men that have stolen our dignity and hurt us." You should know me by now that I will not let you off that easy. The 21 Principles are about becoming the woman and mother that God created us to be.

I decided to trust God on His proposal to spend a year alone with him. I tested him, and told him to take any man out of my life that was not supposed to be there. Watch out what you ask for. One guy was at the point of talking about a serious, committed relationship with me. If you can imagine, the next day he emailed me and broke off the relationship. He did not even have the decency to call, and I never heard from him again. I also happened to be dating a much younger and splendidly handsome guy at the same time. (I know! Why do you think God told me to stop?) I never heard from him again either. That was enough evidence for me to see it was God, so I committed to a year alone with him. I thought it would be extremely easy; I was terribly wrong.

Since I could not go out on dates anymore, the following Saturday night I stayed home and watched TV. A home shopping program featured their new "Royalty Collection" of jewelry. A beautiful, classic sapphire and diamond ring (fake) came on the screen. I heard the Lord say, *"Buy that for yourself and wear it on your wedding finger."*

When I received it in the mail and put it on I said, "God, who is ever going to ask me out if they see a wedding ring on my finger?" The Lord said, *"That is exactly the point. You are my Bride, and I want you to let everyone know it. Do you seriously think your fake ring will stop my man of God from hearing my voice that you are the woman I created for him?"*

It was hard to spend time alone with God. I did not know God on a personal level then, and I was afraid of him. I was filled with so much guilt and shame that I could not face him. I started to doubt if I genuinely wanted to be his Bride after all.

After committing a year alone with God, I met an incredibly handsome guy while playing tennis. I bought into the enemy's lie that I was dreadfully lonely. I thought it would make me feel better to have dinner with him, so I decided to ask him out. I still did downright stupid things like that because I hated myself. I did not think that any handsome man would ask me out first. I starting walking over to the tennis shop when I heard the Lord say, *"Don't do it Lori."* I could feel the war going on between my flesh and spirit, yet I kept walking. Again I heard the Lord say, *"Don't do it."* I kept walking but my steps became unusually slow for I knew God was talking to me. Then I heard God say, *"Don't you have an affair on me!"* I stopped dead in my tracks and ran back to my car. I hated being alone with God, and I was mad at my self for making this promise. I drove home, got out of the car and slammed the door shut with all my might. Then, I stomped into the house and slammed the garage door too. I screamed at the top of my lungs to God, "Why are you doing this to me? Why are you punishing me like this?" The Lord ever so gently spoke to my spirit and said, *"I'm not punishing you. You have been through so much. You need this time to heal."*

I finally realized how serious God was about me, and how much I truly needed to be alone with him. For the first time, I felt like God loved me so much that he wanted to keep me safe and protect me. From then on, it has been a journey of a lifetime spending time with God.

This time has allowed me to recover from so many damaged emotions. I feel unconditionally loved and accepted now by God. Being alone with him has kept both me and my son safe. I used to get into such crummy relationships with men because I hated my self so much. Now, I love myself and refuse to live beneath the privileges that God has for me. I will *never* settle for anything less than God's best for me as I have done in the past. This time alone with God has allowed Him to restore me from the inside out. I feel ready for a Godly man to come into my life, if that is God's will. If not, I am perfectly satisfied with the husband that I have in God.

 If you are in a relationship right now, I challenge you to evaluate if it is truly God's will. If not, it needs to end and you need to be alone with God for at least one year. If you cannot do this on your own, ask God to take any man out of your life that does not belong there. You might just end up like I did, and find it to be the best experience of your life.

 Every single mom needs to know what unconditional love feels like, and this is something you will never experience from another human being. We are not capable of giving it. You can only experience this unselfish love from God, and that comes from getting to know Him.   Once you experience *intimacy without a physical touch*, you will never let your self be degraded, demoralized, or treated with disrespect again. After experiencing God's love, you will never settle for living beneath your privileges as the Bride of Christ. You will know how it feels to be a Queen to the King of the Universe. You will want, and expect the absolute best of everything for you and your children.

 We love as we have been loved. For so many of us that has not been a positive experience from another human being. When you experience true love from the Father, love like you have never known for others will pour out of you. Do yourself and your children a tremendous favor. Commit a year to be alone with God. I promise that you will love it, and you will never be the same again.

1. **If you are involved with a man right now, what is the motive for the relationship?**
2. **Are you in any way outside of the will of God in this relationship? If so, why do you put yourself in a position like that?**
3. **Would you be willing to end the relationship and be alone with God for at least one year? If not, why?**

54

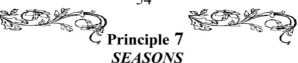

Principle 7
SEASONS

"To everything there is a season, and a time to every purpose under heaven" Ecclesiastes 3:1

It is fall as I write this Principle, and I am in absolute awe of the spectacular colors on the trees. It is hard to believe that early in winter these trees will be barren, empty branches. After the snow melts, spring will be here and little buds will appear on the branches. Summer will be right around the corner, and these trees will be in full bloom with rich green leaves.

Never have I been through so many changes in my life than when I became a single mother. I went from a wife and stay at home mom, to full- time employee and head of the household. For every hat that needed to be worn in taking care of a family I now wore it alone.

I felt that I needed to be both the mom and dad in the family. I now realize that was wrong. God did not make me to be a father. He made me a woman and a mother. In trying to take on fatherhood, a position that I was not meant to represent, I stopped feeling like a woman.

We need to apply the model of the tree to our lives as single mothers. Even though a tree goes through different changes through out the seasons, it still remains a tree. It never tries to take on the part of something that it is not. This tree never tries to become a flower, plant or shrub. With all of the changes we go through as single mothers the only part we are to perform is that of a woman and mother. Trying to be a father goes against what scripture says in Genesis 2:23, **"She shall be called woman, because she was taken out of Man."** God has blessed us with two extraordinarily beautiful qualities; a woman and mother. They will always remain the same, no matter how many more changes we go through. It is essential to remember that being a single mom is a season in your life right now. We need to focus on what we should be doing as a single mother, not on what we think might be missing in our lives right now.

God gives us two beautiful examples in His word of what he wants women to be doing. The first is Titus 2:3-5 that says, **"Likewise, teach the older women to be reverent in the way they live, not to be slanderers or addicted to much wine, but to teach what is good. Then they can train the younger women to love their husbands and children, to be self-controlled and pure, to be busy at home, to be kind, and to be subjected to their husbands, so that no one will malign the word of God."** When I first read this verse the one word I originally had trouble grasping was "husband." I know, however, from the Principle of the Wedding that God is my husband.

What this verse meant to me is that I should be working on my Christ like character, and not spending time gossiping or doing the bar scene. Every thing that I say and do needs to have a positive impact on my son.

A single mom must also crucify her flesh of sexual desires, and relish in God as her husband. We are sexual beings, yet God's plan of sex is for marriage only. *It is not for you as a single mom!* I seriously struggled in this area for a long time until I finally asked God to turn off the sexual button in me. He did what I asked him to do, and now the rest was up to me to control my mind. I could not allow any sexual thoughts in. I had to stop listening to any music that was sexual (good-by Barry White) or that had sexual comments (No more Bad Company, "Feel like making love"). I also had to stop watching love story movies like "The Notebook" and any romance scenes on television.   A single mom should be busy taking care of her children and home with a clear understanding that God is the head of her household. When you live like this God will not be dishonored. You will create a glorious example of Christ to your children and others.

The second example of what God wants women doing is found in **Proverbs 31:10-31**. When you read through these verses, notice that a husband is not found in the picture of what this woman is doing. Let's take a look at what her priorities are, and what we can relate to in our lives as a single mother.

1. Her first priority is her relationship with God. A healthy single mom commits to her spiritual growth. As the Spiritual Leader of her home, she puts God's word in her and her children. She acknowledges God as her husband, and the head of her home. When we clearly understand we are the Bride of Christ we will be faithful to God and live out our days serving Him.

2. Her next priority is her children. A healthy single mom commits to training up her children to become spiritual warriors for Christ. They need to see that God is first in their mom's life, and that they are second. A man in your life should *never* have second place in your priorities until your wedding day.

She is always looking for ways to make her children feel special and valuable. When my son got his first email address, he loved going to the computer to hear, "You've got mail" where he found an email from me. We need to let our children know that they are loved, accepted, and significant in our eyes.

3. Her next priority is her home. A healthy single mom commits to making home happen. I just love what Elizabeth George said in her book, "Beautiful in God's Eyes" that my job as a woman and mother is to light up my home with sparkle, no matter how tough times are. I am to bring the joy, life, love and nourishment to my home and set a worthy example of a woman. My home needs to be an example of heaven on earth. When my son walks through our door, he is assured that home is a safe place from the world. It is the place where all of his needs are met. A single mom needs to watch over every facet of her home. She needs to know everything that is going on in her home and the lives of her children. This includes checking what music they are listening to, what they are watching on TV and who are they hanging out with. Women have eyes in the back of their head, so use them.

4. Her next priority is herself. A healthy single mom takes care of herself and always looks her best. We need to take care of ourselves spiritually, emotionally and physically, and willingly do what ever it takes to provide all the needs for our family. We need considerable physical strength to accomplish those tasks. Burn the "comfortable" sweat suit, comb your hair, put on some makeup and neat clothes. Look like you are always ready for Mr. Right to come through your door, because he just might. Do not go out in public without looking right, for you represent God. We are to be an excellent example for Him wherever we go.

5. Her next priority is others. A healthy single mom is over flowing with warmth and kindness.   As you will learn in the Principle of Extension, we need to be on the lookout for ways help others wherever we are. Our ministry is wherever we go. Some one is always in worse shape than you are, so keep your spiritual eyes open to your surroundings. Remember that our children and home are the first priority before committing our time to others.

6. Her next priority is her positive attitude. A healthy single mom lets praise lead the way. One of my favorite songs our worship leader sings is "Praise is what I do." Never stop praising God no matter how deep the valley or how hard the trials. Praise keeps our eyes focused on God;

not the situations we are facing.   When we choose to praise instead of worry, we proclaim that God's hand of favor is upon us, our home and our children.   Praise also makes the enemy pack up and run.

Being a woman and mother is such a beautiful thing. Why would we want to try and be anything else? God created us to be nurturers, caretakers of the home and givers of love and encouragement to others. Do not extinguish the fervor and spirit of what being a woman is truly about by trying to be something you are not.

Seasons come, and seasons go. This season as a single mom too shall pass, and you will move into a new season in the future. No matter how many changes you go through in life, you are and will always be a woman and a mother. These are two precious gifts from God that we should never want to change.

1. **Are you trying to be both the mom and the dad? What changes do you need to make to be only the mother?**
2. **Are your children the most important people in your life right now? If not, why?**
3. **What are some ways to show your children how important they are?**
4. **What are some ways to make your home "Heaven on Earth?" Make a list of some little touches you can do to brighten the environment.**
5. **Describe your Spiritual, Emotional, Physical and Financial Health. Describe two things you can do in each area to become healthier.**

Note: "A Woman After God's Own Heart, Beautiful In God's Eyes" Elizabeth George.

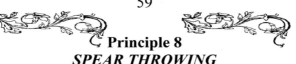

Principle 8
SPEAR THROWING

"I will love those who hurt me. Bless those who curse me and do well to those who hate me." Matthew 5:44

It was Christmas night when I wrote this Principle. My ex-husband picked Eric up that afternoon, and it was the first holiday I spent without my son. As you can imagine, I was not a cheerful woman. I remember thinking, who does he think he is taking my child away from me at Christmas? After all, he was the one who left, and now I am all alone without my son. Boy is he going to pay for this. I took out a sharpening stone to polish up my spear and make it ready for action. All I could think about were the spears thrown at me this year.

There were several of them including the divorce, dealing with the personal challenges of my ex-husbands new wife involved with my son, going back to work, lack of finances, losing my house, my son leaving every other weekend and splitting up the holidays. It seemed utterly ridiculous that spear after spear just kept coming at me.

The Lord showed me what I did with the spears that were thrown at me; I retaliated. I sharpened my spear and threw them right back. I became an expert at spear throwing, and more often than not I used my son as a spear.   I put my son right in the middle of me dealing with his dad.

I would discuss with anyone that would listen to me the things that happened between us. I would share how angry he made me, and what a terrible deed he was doing to both me and my son. The more I talked, the more I hated him. The more I hated him, the more I thought he owed me something for what he did to our family.

I was also stupid enough to try and communicate with my ex-husband in front of my son. There was so much hatred in my heart that it always turned into a shouting match. I became such a master at spear throwing I could throw them with my tongue also. Every chance I had I cut my ex down to others. I cursed his recent marriage, and could not wait for it to fail.

Wow was I mess! Are you doing any of these actions in your life right now with your child's father, or against anyone else? If so, I want to encourage you to go through the Principle of Victory again. Before you can go to the higher places that God has for you, it is imperative that you have a pure heart.

The story in the Bible of David and King Saul is the foundation of this Principle. As you may recall, King Saul was out to kill David, so he ran and hid in a cave. David had the opportunity to kill Saul with his spear, but at the last minute he chose not to.

What is a single mom to do when she has a spear thrown at her? According to Gene Edwards in his book "A Tale of Three Kings," you must first pretend you can not see the spear. Second, you must learn to duck very quickly. Last, you must pretend nothing happened.

You can easily tell if you have been hit by a spear; you turn a deep shade of bitter. David followed three rules that kept him from being hit. One, never learn anything about the fashionable, easily mastered art of spear throwing. Two, stay out of the company of all spear throwers. Three, keep your mouth tightly closed. In this way, spears will never touch you, even when they pierce your heart."

What happens when a single mom acts like David instead of King Saul? According to Gene Edwards the answer is you get stabbed to death. What you may say? That is just not fair. Where is the justice in that? What is the good in being speared by this person who is just like

King Saul?" The answer to that question is that you have your eyes on the wrong King Saul.

As long as you look at the person you think is acting like King Saul, you will blame them for your present hell. Be careful for God has his eyes fastened sharply on another King Saul. Not the visible one standing up there throwing spears at you. No, God is looking at another King Saul. One just as bad or worse; God is looking at the King Saul in you. Hopefully, all you can say is Ouch!

How can a single mom make the turn around from being like King Saul to becoming like David? The power of the Holy Spirit and the word of God is what will change you. Ask God to come into your life and change your heart. Then fill your mind with Matthew 5:44 that says, **"I will love those who hurt me, bless those who curse me and do good to those who hate me."**

God was testing me in this Principle late one night. I was putting my son to bed when I heard a hellish pound on my door. I could not guess who would come to my house at 9:00 at night. I peered out thru the side window of the door to see the Sheriff standing there. My heart raced as I opened the door. In a rough voice he told me to sign the papers he had. I just got served with custody papers from Eric's dad. Just then Eric came down the stairs and saw the Sheriff. As I closed the door, Eric asked in a panicked voice what the sheriff wanted.

You can only imagine what was running through my mind and poor little Eric's. Both of us were horrified. I quickly ran to the phone and called my Pastor. I told him what happened, and put myself under the accountability with him in regards to this Principle. I had to make sure I did not learn anything about the fashionable art of spear throwing and retaliate back. This Principle is all about guarding your heart, and that is exactly what I was going to do.

I made a decision to love Eric's dad unconditionally regardless of what just happened. I had to love the sinner and hate the sin. The only people I decided to speak with about this were my Pastor and wise counsel. I learned from the past that the more I talked about a situation, the angrier I became. I had to keep quiet and apply Proverbs 26:20 to my life that says, **"For lack of wood the fire goes out, and where there is no whisperer, contention quiets down."** I choose to forgive him just as Jesus forgave those that nailed him to the cross. He said, **"Father, forgive them, for they do not know what they are doing."** (Luke 23:34)

It was also imperative not to tell Eric what was happening. I did not want to fill his little heart with any bitterness towards his dad. Now this does not mean that I buried my emotions and denied what happened. I was mad, hurt and angry. I chose to put my emotions under control instead of letting them control me. I knew I had to keep my heart as pure as possible.

Next, I started to pray for Eric's dad, and spoke blessings over him on a daily basis. I think I pray harder for him now more than ever. The Lord directed me to ask everyone in my church to write him a letter saying they were praying for him. Some people even invited him to our church. That was an extremely difficult task for me to do. I did it because I knew that God was looking at the King Saul in me.

I tried my best to be polite and considerate to him as if nothing ever happened. (I failed miserably but I tried) It was vital to keep the harmonious relationship with him that we had in the past, regardless of the current situation. This does not mean that I did not establish safe boundaries. My family was just attacked, and I had to protect my son and myself. I will not tolerate sin or abuse against me in any way.

A valuable lesson I learned in this process was to trust God to bring about the justice in my life. The Bible says that God will establish and resolve the cases for His children. I did not have to pay Eric's dad back for the wrong that he did to us. God is Jehovah-Nissi, my banner and my victory, and he will fight the battle for me. This took an enormous amount of faith on my part. As single moms, we must always take the high road and respond in love, then watch what God will do. If you do things God's way and live by the truth of His word instead of our own emotions and feelings, God will fight the battle for you. In the long run you will come out much better.

I had to continually remind myself that God was in control of this court case. Instead of focusing on what was going on in the natural, I had to remember this was just a test. I knew that if I kept my mind under control, and not let bitterness creep in, victory and promotion were waiting for me. I wanted to pass the test instead of going around the same old sorry mountain of anger and resentment.

At stake though was the possibility of loosing my son for two nights a week. It also meant losing my income from not being able to travel and speak during the summer. If I left town during the week to minister, I had to have Eric back home those two nights to spend at his dads. It would be so easy to become extremely bitter. I admit that at first fear, confusion and anger controlled me. My wise counsel provided a shoulder to cry on along with several boxes of tissues.

It was imperative that I stay focused while preparing this court case. I tried to keep my mouth shut, and let God be my vindicator. I had to keep doing the right thing which was follow Matthew 5:44; not return evil for evil. I made the decision, which seemed impossible to do at the time, to extend mercy and keep responding in love. All because I knew that God was looking at the King Saul in me.

Every time a new spear came from this court case I read Psalm 91:5 that says, **"You will not be afraid of the terror by night or of the arrow that flies by day."** I had to reach the point of my faith where I did not get upset and pay Eric's dad back for what he was doing. I also could not attempt to manipulate the situation in any way. I kept on declaring in faith that God is my Jehovah Nissi, my Banner and my Victory. He has already ordained the steps and put the right judge in charge. God already knew the outcome of this court case. I took in several deep breaths, and while exhaling I told myself that everything was going to be alright.

When difficult situations occur with people, always remember that it is just a test. God is only trying to get the King Saul out of you. This builds your character, and sets you up for promotion. Remember, the greater the struggle the greater the reward.

Let me share with you how God brought justice to me in this court case. I was frightened because I did not have the money to pay for an attorney. While praying in the middle of the night the Lord told me that he was my vindicator, and I was not to hire a lawyer. When I shared this with my mentors they said that I should never go into a court room without one. I knew that I heard from God not to hire one, so by faith I went into court representing myself. You will not believe what happened.

I happen to live in the most liberal county in Georgia (remind me to move soon). In a liberal, secular court system I got a Christian judge. Not only did I get a Christian judge, I got a judge that went to seminary. My ex's lawyer got up and read a list of lie's a mile long about me. He also claimed I was using my son as a marketing tool for this ministry. He thought that having Eric on the 21Principles video series or taking him with me to speak was detrimental to him. He also brought up that I try to take Eric to church on the weekends that he was with his dad. Eric wanted to go to church, and my ex said that it intruded on their time together.

After the judge heard both sides of the story, he said there was one consistent word he heard in the courtroom that day, and that word was God. He told Eric's dad that if he could make a new law, he would make him take Eric to church on Sundays. By law though the Judge had to give him one night during the regular week that Eric would sleep over at his house. He also by law had to redefine our summertime schedule, which would still inconvenience me from traveling and speaking. That day in court was the most humiliating and degrading process I have ever been through. I cried the rest of the day and night that he did this to me, and said all of those horrible things about me. Yet, I still had to make a decision not to harbor bitterness and forgive him.

I tried to do the best I could at my part, and God showed up in a mighty way. Just a couple of months after court, out of the blue Eric's dad stopped making him sleep over at his house. He said that he did not want Eric's sleep disturbed for school. He also cancelled the restrictions on me for the summer. I am now able to travel and take Eric with me. My ex also said that he would work around my schedule in any way that was convenient for me.

All of these trials or spears that we face are undoubtedly a test from God. He wants to see where your heart is at. Are you a King Saul or are you a David? A single mom has to keep a positive attitude when spears are thrown at her. Every spear that comes your way is nothing but an opportunity for God to bless you. If you are wise enough to say, "No problem" and refuse to get bitter and angry, you are closer to victory and promotion than you think.

God chose David to do something extraordinary, and he has the same plan for you. We cannot go to the higher places that God has for us with bitterness, anger and un-forgiveness in our hearts. God wants to put you in a position of honor and leadership, but he can not do this until you pass the test. David never got hit by a spear because he knew these three things. Never learn anything about the fashionable art of spear throwing. Stay out of the company of all spear throwers and keep your mouth tightly shut. That way, spears will never touch you even when they pierce your heart.

1. Have you been hit by a Spear? How can you tell that you have been hit?
2. How can you take the high road in the situation?
3. How can you apply David's secret to the situation?
4. Go back through the Workbook in Principle 3 on forgiveness.

Note: "A Tale of Three Kings," Gene Edwards; "Your Best Life Now," Joel Osteen.

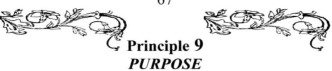

Principle 9
PURPOSE

"Where there is no vision, the people perish"   Proverbs 29:18

At the end of every year, I spend one day alone to meditate on a very important question. My answers then determine the course of my life for the next year, and every step that I take in it. The one question I ask myself is, "What is important about life to me?" This one question is not an easy one to answer. Yet, it is one that needs to be addressed if you are truly going to be a healthy single mom living a life of purpose and meaning, focus and order, balance and harmony.

When I first became a single mom, I experienced the death of a dream. All of my hopes and dreams for the future came to a crushing end in a brief moment of time. I lost all hope because I lost my dream. With nothing to look forward to I went into a deep depression. The Bible says in Proverbs 29:18, **"Where there is no vision, the people perish."** That is exactly what I was doing in this new life as a single mom; perishing.

This new life seemed to be nothing but "horrible" to me. I was upset, alone and overwhelmed with all that I had to do on my own. I could not begin to imagine that life as a single mom would ever get any better. I thought that this was the way life was just going to have to be. Life for me as a single mom was nothing but mere survival. It was all I could do to get through one day, and pray for the strength to get up the next day and do it again. With that manner of thinking, nothing was ever going to change, or get better any time soon. As long as I thought that nothing good would come out of this life as a single mom, then nothing would. If I did not think this so called "mess" of a life as a single mom would ever turn around for the better, then it never would. If I thought I would never be able to reach the dreams I once had for my future now living as a single mom now, then I never would.

The verse in Proverbs 29:18 says that I am to have a vision; a vision of success and not defeat. Do you remember the verse we studied in the Principle of Hope, from Jeremiah 29:11? It said, **"For I know the plans I have for you, plans to prosper you, not to harm you, plans to give you a hope and a future?"** That verse clearly states that we are not to live as a single mom lost, and void of dreams of the future.

When one dream dies we need to conceive a new dream. This comes from the very essence of what is deep down inside of you. They are all of the things that are immensely valuable about life to you.

Having a vision means being able to see something ahead of you. I needed to "see" myself as cheerful, successful and complete as a single mom. We must start looking at life as a single mom through the "eyes of faith." We need to see ourselves rising above the many challenges we face, and living out the best life ever regardless of our circumstances.

What do you want your future to look like? Can you see your dreams being accomplished? Are you focusing on the result? Or do you keep your eyes on the constant challenges that are in the way of reaching your goal? I spent far too many years thinking that as soon as I could get another husband, then I will be joyful again. That form of thinking is wrong.

Open up your mind and consider a new dream; one of success, victory, wealth and happiness as a single mom.

This may require stretching your imagination to see beyond the struggles you feel right now.   Isaiah 54:2 says, **"Enlarge the place of your tent; stretch out the curtains of your dwellings, spare not; lengthen your cords and strengthen your pegs."** Once you have a different picture in front of you, and you genuinely believe that it can happen absolutely nothing will be able to keep you down.

Once you know what is important about life to you, and why it is essential, you will begin to determine the right strategy to live that life.   Then you will move the way you need to, and do the right things in order to achieve your objective.   That is what it means to live a life of Purpose and Meaning.

Once you know what is important about life to you, chaos turns into order. You become effective which means doing all of the right things in order to reach your goals.   It also means you have a reason for everything that you do.   You understand why you are doing it, rather than just doing something. That is what it means to live a life of Focus and Order.

Once you know what is important about life to you; life works! You thrive instead of strive.   You reap great rewards of living out what is relevant to you.   There is joy and peace in your life when you live out your dreams. That is what it means to live a life of Balance and Harmony.

Dreaming your own dream, and making a way to live it out is not selfish.   Your hopes and dreams are seeds that God has already planted in your heart.

The basis of this Principle is to learn how to write out a Life Plan, and then live it out. The first step in designing a life plan is to create an epitaph.   This is what you would want people to remember you by after you leave this world. I wrote my epitaph to read, "Lori lived to serve God, so that no woman would leave this earth saying, "I just never knew.""

After writing my epitaph, I realized that I was not doing two of the most crucial things that were important about life to me. I wanted to spend more time with my son, and teach single mothers the things God has taught me.

I never want a woman to leave this world without going through the Principles of Identity, and Victory. My other desire is for every woman in the world to know about the beautiful design that God created for us to be. Once I realized what was important about life to me, I made plans to quite my corporate job and build this ministry. I am not saying that you should also do something that drastic. You will be amazed though at the changes you will begin to make in your life to live out your God given purposes.

If you are not sure what is essential about life to you, it may help to read Proverbs 31:10-31. God gives us a magnificent example about the woman He designed us to be in these scriptures. This may also give you fresh ideas to model your life around.

I want to challenge you to take a day off and use that time to think and pray about one question, "What is important about life to you?" and then create a Life Plan by doing the following:

1. Make a list of the things in your heart about what is genuinely important about life to you.
2. For every item on your list, write a paragraph that is an exceptionally detailed description of what you see for your self in that life.
3. Narrow the paragraph down to one sentence about why that is important to you.
4. Create a list of some daily activities that you can incorporate into your life to help you live out that vision.

God has so much more in store for you, so open your mind and heart to let God do something new in your life. The Bible says in Matthew 9:17, **"Neither do men pour new wine into old wineskins. If they do, the skins will burst, the wine will run out and the wineskins will be ruined. No, they pour new wine into new wine skins, and both are preserved."** Are you ready to defend your sanity? If so, make a decision to bury the past and start dreaming of something new. God wants to fill your life with new dreams, but first you must be willing to get rid of the old wine skins.

Enjoy your day off and time alone creating a new life plan. Bring your life plan, a daily calendar and some blank paper with you as you turn the page to Principle 10, "The Hourglass." I will teach you how to make your life plan work for you.

Create your Life Plan according to the outline on page 70.

PART TWO

FOCUS AND ORDER

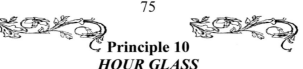

Principle 10
HOUR GLASS

Commit your works to the Lord and your plans will be established.
Proverbs 16:3

My favorite movie I used to love watching with my son is Disney's, "Aladdin." The scene I can relate to most is near the end of the movie where Princess Jasmine was captured and put into an hour glass. The sand is pouring down on her and rapidly surrounding her body. Her precious time is ticking away, and soon she will be buried to death. Suddenly, Aladdin smashes the hour glass open and sets her free from captivity. My desire for you in this Principle is to set you free from the insanity of running against time.

I felt like Princess Jasmine when I became a single mom. No, not rich and beautiful, but helpless from all I had to do in one day by myself. I never finished what needed to be done, and the things left undone kept piling up on top of me. I was doing so many things, but never the ones I truly needed to do.

With all of the activities our children are involved in, we need to be cloned several times to get one child to one place, and pick up the others. It is vital to have a network of other single moms and families to help you out. It does not require a village, just a few close friends that genuinely want to help you.

In the Principle of Purpose, we learned how a life plan will help you determine what is important about life to you. The Principle of the Hourglass will teach you how to make your life plan work for you. There are three important items you need for this Principle; your life plan, a calendar that shows a daily time frame and some blank pieces of paper.

The three areas we are going to cover in this Principle are:
1. Discover where you do not make the best use of time.
2. How to do only the things that are important to you.
3. How to have fun doing it.

God has given us all the same amount of time in each day. It is essential to value this gift of twenty four hours, and glorify God with every minute of it. Becoming a successful single mom is similar to playing chess. Every move you make must be calculated and purposeful. Each step that you take connects for a purpose that builds momentum for you. This momentum, purpose, and grace of God will make you more than a conqueror in your daily activities.

When Eric was younger he loved going to the circus. He still remembers the time I surprised him and took him to the Barnum and Bailey show. He also loves to remind me that he threw up in the garage when we got home from eating too much cotton candy and popcorn. My son was fascinated by the lion tamer and wondered why he used a stool. It turns out that it is for the lion tamers safety. When the lion tries to focus on all four feet of the stool at the same time, it paralyzes the lion and makes it weak.

My life felt like a three ring circus when I became a single mom. The same analogy of the lion and stool could be applied to my life. When I looked ahead at all that I had to do in one day on my own, I often broke down in tears. It seemed impossible that I could actually get everything done. I often found myself paralyzed like the lion looking at all four legs of the stool at the same time. The day usually ended with me hardly doing anything at all.

When I shared my frustration with a friend of mine, she suggested I keep track of how I spent my life for two weeks straight. I did it and discovered I wasted so much time doing things that certainly did not need to be done at that time. I also neglected the most valuable things like spending time with my son, and taking proper care of my self.

I want to encourage you to keep track of how you spend your time for two weeks straight. Get a note pad and keep it with you at all times to indicate how you spend a twenty four hour period. After the two weeks are up, match your record up to your life plan. See if you are doing the things that are truly important about life to you, or if you are settling for second best.

There are two secrets of a successful single mom. They are to think and do things in order of priorities. Your life plan will help you to acknowledge your priorities, and the Principle of the Hourglass will help you to control your priorities.

Why is it necessary to live by our priorities? It turns chaos into order. There is so much pressure in our lives, and we only have a certain amount of time to do so many things. We have to learn to say "yes" to the best which are the priorities in your life plan, and "no" to the rest. The best is what is important about life to you. ***If it is not on your life plan do not do it!***

I used to blame my lack of time on all that I had to do as a single mom. Granted we have a lot to do, but I discovered that I am my own worst enemy. I was constantly frustrated trying to capture time, when what I actually needed to do was overcome myself. Victory came by making my self do the things I had to do when it needed to be done. I also had to do these things even when I did not feel like doing them. This keeps you organized and in control of your life instead of it controlling you.

Organization is the power that allows you live with a sense of purpose. There is balance and harmony in your day instead of chaos. When you know what you have to do and when you have to do it, a force gets started that continues on through out the day. You get on a roll, and one by one the projects get done.

When we act as the Bible says, **"To work unto the Lord,"** it puts a whole new perspective on how you spend God's time. I believe that my son has a renewed sense of pride for me because of my move management process. He sees things getting done, and the real reward of hard work and focus. It is enjoyable going through your day with a sense of pride knowing you are accomplishing something, rather than living in defeat and confusion.

I am going to take you through this simple exercise to help you make your life plan work for you by putting it into action.

1. First, take your sheet of blank paper and at the top of it write down your first priority from your life plan. Then underneath that priority write the numbers 1,2,3,4, in list fashion, one under the other. Try not to have more than three or four things under each priority. It is OK to have only one or two. Remember, we are working on only the main things that are essential about your life.

2. Second, write down all of the things that need to be done for that priority.

3. Third, prioritize your list. What is going to get done first, second, third and fourth?

4. Fourth, organize each priority. What do you want to prepare for that certain project? Make an ABC list under each project and prioritize it.

5. Fifth, determine how much time you need to do each item. Then, put it on your daytime sheet at what time you are going to do it.

6. Sixth, make sure that you do it.

For example, my first Priority in my life plan is God. So I ask myself, "What do I want to do with God today?" I know that I want to pray and read God's word today. So my subtitle would be God. Then I make my 1, 2, 3 and 4 list. Number one would be pray, number two would be read God's word and so on. Before you move on, prioritize this list.

Then I ask myself about number one; what is crucial about prayer to me today? I list these things under prayer in 1, 2, 3, 4 order and prioritize my list. Number one is my personal time with God. Number two is my prayer time with Eric. Number three is prayer with my prayer partner. Number four is prayer time with my women's group. Next to each one of these items I put what I need for the project in A, B, C order. In this instance of prayer, A is my prayer journal, B is making a prayer list for that day and C is my Bible. So my sheet will look like this for prayer.

Prayer:

1. Personal alone time with God
    A. Journal
    B. Prayer List
    C. Bible
2. Prayer with Eric
    A. Prayer list
    B. Prayer Outline
3. Prayer with my prayer partner
    A. Journal
    B. Prayer list
4. Prayer with others
    A. Prayer list
    B. Journal

The next step is to resolve when to do them, and how long it will take. My personal prayer time is in the morning from 5:00 am-6:00am, again from 12:00-12:15, and at 10:15-10:30. I put the word prayer on my calendar at the designated times. The Bible says to pray always, so we need to pray all through out our day. Next, my prayer time with Eric is from 7:30-7:40 before school, so I write that in my calendar. My time with my prayer partner is Friday at 10:00-10:30, so I write that in my calendar. My scheduled time to pray with others is Tuesday nights from 7:00pm-8:30, so I write that in my calendar. My scheduled time with my women's group is Tuesday from 10:00-12:00, so I write that in my calendar. Now it is just a matter of starting and stopping each project at the described time.

Now wasn't that easy? It is just as effortless as doing that for all the rest of your life's priorities. Watch how the calendar will fill up, but also observe how it will fill up with the meaningful things in your life. Remember, this is what you determined how you wanted to live your life, so live it!

The beauty of this is when you get bombarded with things that you *could* be doing, you are already set on the things that you *should* be doing. This will save you from doing things that are not on your priority list. Distraction is a leading tactic of Satan. He does not want you to be focused and organized. He wants you to live in frustration and chaos. This move management system will also help you identify an attack from the enemy.

Another form of interference comes in the form of phone calls and text messages. How many times have you sat down to dinner to enjoy some time with your children and the phone rings or the text messages come? Eric used to sneak his cell phone to the dinner table and text his friends from under the table. When I caught him doing that, he tried pretending he was getting something out of the refrigerator, so he could send a text from behind the open door. Our dinner got interrupted, and I lost valuable time with my son.

If a call does come in, screen it to see if it is an emergency. If the phone happens to get answered during dinner, or your alone time with the children, it is alright to tell the person that you are with your children right now, and that you would be delighted to call them back later. This is not being rude to the person on the phone. It is honoring your children to show them how much you love and respect them, and the precious time that you have with them.

This also lets your children know where they fit into your priorities. They should be second place only to God. Again, no man in your life should *ever* be number two until the preacher pronounces you husband and wife.

Eric learned at an exceptionally young age to stop asking me if I was going to answer the phone when it rang if we were doing something together. I told him my time with him was more valuable than the person on the other end of the phone. He just smiled and hugged me for he felt so loved and valued. I know the other person on the phone may be loved and valued too, but not in the same priority that our children are.

I hope that you have enjoyed filling in your calendar with what is important about life to you. I pray that you have a different outlook on life, and a sense of peace knowing that you can get things done.

Remember these basic steps:
1. List the Priority.
2. List all that needs to be done under each Priority 1,2,3,4.
3. Prioritize the list.

4. Organize each project, what needs to be done to achieve this goal in A, B, C order.
5. Decide how much time you need to do each task.
6. Put in on the calendar at the time you are going to do it
7. Then do it!

Always work according to the way you function best. If you are a morning person do your hard work in the morning. If you are a night person do you easiest work in the morning.

It is also beneficial to fill in the little gaps of time. I always have a Bible, a book, some learning CDs and a tape recorder in the car with me. This is a terrific way to learn while driving. When caught in traffic jams or car pool line, I can always read or register thoughts for a new series or book that I am writing.

It is also a brilliant plan to have something in your purse that you can read. I'm amazed at how much time we spend standing in lines waiting at stores. Instead of reading the trashy magazines that beg for our attention at the checkout lines, memorize your "Who Am I in Christ" statements found in Principle 2. Keep the 21Principles book in your purse at all times.

If you did not finish a particular project because your time limit was up, use these gaps to go back and finish. Just the other day I had to stop cleaning the bathroom because my time frame was up (What a shame!). I allotted myself twenty minutes to clean, and at 7:20 pm my time was up. It was not the end of the world that the bathroom was not finished. I did not have people coming over that night that may have used it, so I moved on to my next project. The next day I finished something before the time I allowed, and used those extra minutes to complete the bathroom. You can also use these gaps to organize a drawer or assemble things for meals in the days ahead. Children will also benefit from having their own time schedule. This will teach them ample organization skills for their future, and give them a sense of accomplishment. It will also make things easier on you because they will learn to be more responsible for themselves.

When Eric was younger he had his own journal with thirty one tabs in it; one for each day of the month. In it was his list of chores broken down by each day that he had to finish. He knew what was expected of him in the morning, after school and evening. This also included his personal Bible study, and reading he did each day. After fulfilling his daily responsibilities, he signed his sheet and gave it to me. If he completed his daily assignments, he got to pick something he wanted to do for our family fun time. Now that he is older and running his own pet service, everything is on his smart phone. This has unquestionably taught him discipline, move management skills, and the rewards of personal responsibility, hard work and dedication.

You may wonder, "How do I have fun doing everything while staying on track?" The answer lies in a timer of some kind. My son and I make doing the things we need to do fun by turning it into a game. We all know that children love games and it is fun for me too. We play the game called "Beat the clock."

When Eric was younger and had a chore to do, I would ask him how fast he thought he could get it done. That way he took personal ownership of his project. He would laugh and give me a time frame. I would set the timer and off he went to beat the clock. We also did this with things we had to do together. It helped us develop strong teamwork skills, all while trying to beat a certain time frame together. We laughed, encouraged each other along the way and had a lot of fun. This was extremely useful for projects that we *did not* want to do, for it turned dread into fun. We also thought of a small bonus we would get if we beat the clock. Things went smooth and easy when we approached the things that we had to do with a "let's have fun" attitude. Even though Eric is a teenager now, this still works sometimes for who can pass up a fun game. It is surprising how he will to this day choose to do his work with a good attitude. I still do this for myself even today with a teenager, for it helps me get things done.

When you work in small chunks of time like this, it keeps you focused on the present. You will not become paralyzed or weak from looking ahead at everything that is still left to do. Learn to appreciate the present; what you are doing at the time you are doing it. When that project or block of time is over, it is over. Move on to the next one and plan ahead of time to enjoy it, and have fun doing it.

Single moms cannot run the pattern of time for it proceeds consistently and constantly. I hope this Principle of the Hourglass has shattered the pressures you face in managing your time, and will help you strategically and purposefully manage your moves.

Remember to say "no" to anything that is not on your list of what's important about life to you. That way you will always live life to the fullest from your point of view, and not settle for anything less than God's best.

1. Design a minute by minute plan for the day starting with your Life Priorities.
2. Fill in the gaps of time.
3. Fill out a daily calendar this way for the week, then the month.

Note: "Developing the Leader With In You," John Maxwell

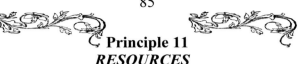

Principle 11
RESOURCES

"He who trusts in his riches will fall, but the righteous will flourish like the green leaf." Proverbs 11:28

The greatest challenge I believe single mothers face is the lack of finances. This often leads to much fear and anxiety in our lives. Along with every challenge, is the opportunity to grow and prosper in the circumstances life deals us.

My time of greatest growth came from the lack of finances when I became a single mom. I think it was the exact thing that God took away from me to force me closer to Him. Some times we have to come down to the end of our own resources before we can experience God's. It took my checkbook, refrigerator and pantry being empty to see who God truly is to me as a single mom. He is Jehovah-Jireh my provider as the Bible says in Genesis 22:14, **"So Abraham called that place The Lord Will Provide. And to this day it is said, "On the mountain of the Lord it will be provided."**

The name Jehovah-Jireh means, "The Lord Who Sees" or, "Jehovah's Provision Shall Be Seen." God knows and sees our needs before hand, and makes provisions for them. God knows that you and your children need to eat and have a place to live. The Bible also says that food, clothing and shelter are all that we need.

I never knew how delightful just the basics were until I was forced to live that way after becoming a single mom. Going from my dream home in an exceptionally nice neighborhood to a small little apartment was not my notion of a good life. What the Lord showed me during that time was life changing. I was able to see where I made a false idol out of money, and how I was a slave to materialism.

It is true what the Bible says that we cannot serve two masters.

Simplicity is a remarkably pleasant thing. I found it truly astonishing how close I became to God when I had extremely little both materially and financially. There was nothing to get in the way of my relationship with Him. It drove me to totally rely and trust in God for everything that we needed. It was not until I was out of everything materially and financially that I realized earthly things failed me every time I put my trust in them.

God never failed me though; especially when I needed Him the most. All I could do was open my empty pantry and just speak the name of God. I just looked at the empty shelves and said, "Jehovah-Jireh please provide for us."

I was expecting money to come so I could buy groceries. God provided my needs through other people that He sent to take care of us. This situation happened because my paycheck was seven days late in the mail. I lived paycheck to paycheck, penny to penny at the time. I thought this was the worst problem I ever had.

For seven days straight people called "out of the blue" and invited us over to dinner, out to a restaurant or just felt led to bring something over to our house and have a meal together. None of those people had any inkling I was penniless. I ended up having ample food in my refrigerator from the leftovers, and doggy bags from the restaurants.

Never was I without when I trusted that God is who He said he is, and that he would provide for us. A single mom can be at peace when the resources are few or gone. God wants us to completely rely on Him for everything that we need, and trust that he will provide. During this time the Lord taught me three simple things to do with my (His) money. This helped me to make sure I always had what I needed, and I want to share them with you in this Principle.

The first thing the Lord told me to do was tithe the money He provided for me. The Bible says in Malachi 3:10, **"Bring the whole tithe into the storehouse, that there may be food in my house. Test me in this," says the Lord Almighty, "and see if I will not throw open the floodgates of heaven and pour out so much blessing that you will not have room enough for it."** I was so afraid to tithe, for I was spending my entire pay check just to live from moment to moment. While reading my Bible one night I came upon this passage from Mark 12:41-44 that says, **"And he sat down opposite the treasury, and began observing how the people were putting money into the treasury; and many rich people were putting in large sums. A poor widow came and put in two small copper coins, which amount to a cent. Calling his disciples to Him, He said to them, "Truly I say to you, this poor widow put in more than all the contributors to the treasury. For they all put in out of their surplus, but she, out of her poverty, put in all she owned, all she had to live on."** At that moment I told God that I would test him on this, and made the decision to tithe. If I did not have what I needed after tithing, I decided to be like Esther in the Bible and say, "If I perish, I perish." What was the worst thing that could happen to me if God said to test him? On Sunday morning I made out my tithe check and put it in the offering. I had no concept of how God was going to provide for the utility bills coming up, but He did. I received an unexpected bonus from work that week that covered the bills and then some. I tithed the bonus check, and I am here to say that I have never been without for what I need. I also have extra to bless others. If I wrote down all the provisions God made for me because of my tithe, there would not be enough pages to record them. I want to challenge you today to "just do it," and test God with your tithe.

All of our resources come *from* God, and they all belong *to* God. He is our source, and what we have from Him are his resources. The way we use the money God gives us reveals a lot about our character. God is asking us to give back ten percent, or the first fruits, of the resources He provides for us. This will prove that we put God first in our lives.

God wants us to give Him the first, and the best of everything we receive. (This includes child support and gifts) What we do first with God's money shows what we value most. When we give our tithe, it immediately focuses our attention on God. It also reminds us that all we have belongs to Him. Our tithe is a natural response to love, and our giving proves that our love towards God is real. God says to "bring the full tithe into the storehouse." and that means the first ten percent goes to your church.

It is so easy to be deceived that money will provide security for us as single moms. There are too many ways for money to lose its power. It can be stolen from us, inflation takes away its value, a recession can come along and we lose our jobs, or the stock market crashes. God never looses His power though. He is always faithful and dependable. We need to look to God solely to provide our safety and security.

Money has the ability to take the role of God in our life. With all of the needs we have in being a single mom, it can become your master. You can tell if you have become a slave to money if you think and worry about money all the time, if you are in debt, if it is difficult for you to give money away, if you give up what you should be doing in order to make more money, and if you spend too much time caring for your possessions.

If we cannot honor God by giving Him back the ten percent he requires, how can he possibly bless us with more money in the future? God is asking us to be faithful stewards of his provisions. Do not let your integrity fall in this small matter, and it will not disappoint you in critical matters down the road. The Bible says in Luke 12:33, **"For where your treasure is, there your heart will be also."** Show God today that he is the number one priority in your life by giving back to His Kingdom through your tithe.

Point One: Do what ever it takes to give back to God ten percent of the resources that He has provided for you.

The second thing the Lord led me to do was handle my resources properly by living off of a budget. That way I could keep track of how I spent Gods money. Having a budget also taught me management skills, and discipline to make sure that everything my son and I needed would be provided for. I had to learn to live within my means and not rob Peter to pay Paul. By living from a budget I could always make sure that our physical needs were met, not just our desires. I also chose to live off the system that if I could not pay cash for it, I could not have it. I do not use credit cards, and I no longer have any debt.

In order to create a realistic, working budget I kept track of every single penny I spent for two months. This helped me to see where my money was actually going. I was then able to separate my monthly income out appropriately to different categories starting with my tithe. The rest of the categories were prioritized as follows: taxes, housing, food, car, insurance, debts, recreation/entertainment, clothes, savings, medical expenses, miscellaneous, investments, school and daycare. I assigned each group a dollar amount based off the tracking I did in the past two months. The secret to running a successful budget is when the money in the category is gone it is gone for the month. There is no robbing from one group to substitute another.

Point Two: Live off of a Budget

The last thing the Lord spoke to me about was to balance my checkbook daily. It is too easy to use your debit card or write a check, and fail to remove the amount from the balance. When you need the money, it is not there if things have not been recorded correctly. If you have ever bounced a check, you understand the fees charged against you could easily equal a weeks worth of groceries.

When you know your daily balance, it gives you peace about where you are at financially. You are not worried about how you are going to put gas in your car or feed your family. You know how much money you have to spend, and that your bills can be paid. I know there are some excellent books out there about money management, but you can never go away from these basics. If you do not have a computer or software package to manage and track your spending, I want to share with you two simple ways to do this.

If you want to work with cash, you can use designated envelopes for each category of your budget to keep your weekly or monthly money in. Put the designated amount into the envelope, and then pay as you go. This may not be the safest way to work though for if you lose it, or if it is stolen, you are out of your money.

Another way to manage your spending is to use your debit card and a pocket notebook. Make a page in the notebook for each category in your budget. Put the name of the category and the designated dollar amount at the top of the page. Then subtract the entire group amount from your check book. Now you can use your debit card for the purchases you need to make in that realm. Immediately subtract each purchase from your original number on the note pad. Make sure and maintain the proper balance after every purchase. At the end of the month, the amount you consume should equal the amount you deducted from your checking account. Hopefully, you will have some left over from your careful management.

For example, when you go grocery shopping and buy food and miscellaneous items such as laundry detergent, and some personal items like shampoo, you can pay for each group separately. Remember to record, and subtract the exact amount in each designated area from your notebook. This will take a little extra time at the cash register, but it is well worth it to keep the budget in balance.

By using one of these methods you are able to keep a record of where you are spending God's money. This will help you make adjustments if you have not budgeted enough in a particular area for what you actually need.

Point 3: Know your balance daily.

I know these times may be difficult for you, and I know exactly what you are going through. Remember that God is who He says He is; he is Jehovah Jireh your provider. If you will do your part, and are in God's will with your tithe and budget, God will do His part to provide everything you need according to His riches and glory.

I want to challenge you to get your financial house in order. Make a commitment to test God and start to tithe. God will not let you go without your needs met when you decide to put Him first in your life. Remember, God is your source, and what you have are His resources. I've heard it said that you can tell where someone's treasure is just by looking at their checking account. Evaluate where you spend your money and match it up to what you have learned about in this Principle. When you are willing to do your part, God will do His.

Make a plan to implement Points 1, 2 and 3 in your life.

Principle 12
COMMUNICATION

"A wicked messenger falls into adversity, but a faithful envoy brings healing."
Proverbs 13:17

We have so little time to spend with our children from all the many responsibilities we bear. It is easy to feel guilty about not having as much quantity time with them as we want. That is why it is vital to be effective with the brief time we do have. For a single mom to be successful with her children, she must understand her own personality style, and those of her children. This way, she can respond to each child in the way they will best receive her. This is achieved by focusing on their strengths, and nurturing their weakness.

My strengths are being an extrovert, a doer and an optimist. The strengths of my emotions are that I am a leader. In my work I am goal oriented. In my parenting style I move my family to action. When it comes to friends, I can thrive with exceptionally few. I also enjoy group activities. My weaknesses are in my emotions for I am easily annoyed. At work I do not analyze details. As a parent I tend to over dominate, and as a friend I can be too independent.

My son, on the other hand, is more the introvert, watcher and pessimist. He is remarkably easy going, relaxed and charming. He can take the good with the bad, and he is exceedingly friendly and enjoyable. His weaknesses are that he can tend to be indecisive. He is not real goal oriented or organized (then again what child is?), and he can tend to be judgmental.

My son and I have a real conflict in personalities. If I am not careful as a mother, I could undoubtedly thwart his personality. I have to tone down my personality a bit to relate to his relaxed, peaceful personality. On the other hand, my personality actually lifts him up to a new degree in leadership and motivation.

I use my knowledge of his weaknesses as a teaching tool to help him. For example, Eric has a hard time making a decision. He has a keen memory and positively hates writing things down. (Oh to be young and invincible!) It would be so much easier on me to just tell him what to do, and at what time to do it. Certainly that would not be preparing him for the future in any way, or help him grow and develop.

When Eric was much younger, I created a program to turn his weakness into strength. I made him a notebook with 1-31 tabs in it representing each day of the month. For every day of the month, I made a list of the things he needed to achieve such as Bible study, chores and walking the dogs. At breakfast we went through his daily sheet together, and he chose what time segment he wanted to do things broken down into morning, afternoon or night. Before he went to bed he signed his sheet and turned it into me. This represented that he did every thing he was supposed to do. If he accomplished his goals for the day, he got rewarded in some way.

Eric is older now, and has so much going on with school, sports, and his own pet sitting business. Technology has made it easier for him to keep track of everything he needs to do. I bought him a smart phone to use instead of the day timer he graduated to after his notebook. Even though he does not have to turn in a daily page, he is experiencing the rewards of being organized on his own.

Three years ago I helped Eric start his own pet sitting service. When a new client wanted to hire him, he arranged a meeting at their house for a consultation, and to meet their pets. Initially I went with him to make sure he was safe, and help him with his business skills.

When we got back home he had to quickly enter the days and time he needed to work on his phone and our family calendar. I also insisted that he use the reminder feature on his phone. This was so difficult to get him to do, for it is a weakness of his. I also designed a sheet for him to leave behind at his client stating the services he performed. He has to check several items off three times a day when he takes care of a pet. Getting him to do this initially was like World War III for me. I knew if I kept helping him develop his weakness, the rewards would be great for him in the future.

He quickly learned the value of using organizational tools. One night he went to bed and forgot to take a pet out for its last walk. He did not use his phone calendar or reminder. I told him about the pet, and he had to go do it and pay me! (I hope his clients are not reading this) Needless to say, he now understands the necessity of planning and is immensely effective with the tools available to him.

Eric's is quite the business man now. His client's praise him on how professional and organized he is, and what a fantastic business he is running. They have told their friends and neighbors about his services, and he is making a lot of money. Now he wants to get his degree in business and have his own company in the future.

There is merit in all of this for he is learning and growing, and it takes the pressure off of me. I do not want to be a nagging, controlling, dominating mother which is a weakness of mine. We discuss it one time, it is on his phone and our family calendar, and that is all that needs to be said. Hopefully his weakness has turned into a real advantage for Eric that will help him to be an effective, mature adult in the future. I just keep telling myself that it is my job to teach him, and pray for my own sanity!

At times I need to talk to Eric about some serious things, and need him to communicate back. What I found works best for him is to do things with him that put him at ease. For example, he loves to throw the baseball and play catch. I will play ball with him and talk about the things we need to discuss. He is extremely open and responsive when relaxed and comfortable. The language he understands is some form of play time. We can play and talk, or we can have fun playing and then sit down and talk. These are exceptional times to spend time with him doing what he wants to do, and we actually get a chance to communicate.

With a clear understanding of our own nature and our children's, we can give them what they need from us. It will also help you make the best use of the short time you have with them. Most people are not just one particular personality type, but a combination of several different ones. That is what makes each person so special.

There is no one set test or personality style that will tell you how to communicate with your child. Only God knows the correct answer to that. After all, he made them and knows exactly what they need. I highly recommend that you pray and ask Him the best way to communicate with your children.

God is the master communicator, and he used some particularly unorthodox methods to communicate with His people. He used angels to speak to Jacob, Zacharias, Mary and the Sheppard's. He used dreams to talk to Joseph, Jacob, a baker, a cupbearer, Pharaoh, Isaiah, Joseph and the Magi. He used writing on the wall to talk to Belshazzar. He used a talking donkey to speak to Balaam. He used a pillar of cloud and fire to talk to the People of Israel. He used a fish to talk to Jonah. He verbally communicated with Abraham, Moses, Jesus at his baptism and Paul. He used fire to speak to Moses. He also uses His son to talk to us through the Holy Spirit and the Bible.

If you do not know how to communicate with your children, ask God to convey the message for you. There are many times I do not know how to get through to Eric, but God does. One time Eric decided he was not going to play tennis anymore, and refused to even pick up his racquet. I could not understand why for he was exceptionally skilled at the game. I asked the Lord what sport he should play instead, and he said it was still to be tennis. Instead of fighting with Eric, I asked the Lord to speak to him about it, and I kept silent. About two months later Eric asked me if he could play in a particular tennis tournament. He said he felt God wanted him to play, and he got right back in the game. I seem to have more luck when I throw my hands up in the air and ask God to handle it for me. Remember, He is your husband and loves to take care of you and help you.

We can also communicate to our children through God's word. If you do not know how to handle a situation, just look up in the Bible what God says about it and **let His word do the talking for you.** After all, God is your child's Father and he knows what His children need. We need to trust God to be the father to the fatherless.

Ask God to guide you how to communicate with each of your children. That is exactly what I did when Eric was exceptionally young, and the Lord said to play with him.

God was right, and that is truly what Eric loves to do when we need to talk. You can also talk with your children directly if they are old enough to understand. Simply tell them you want to make the most out of your time with them. Ask them the best way for you to spend time together that would open the doors for you to talk. What child can resist a parent that wants to know what they truly want and need to spend the best possible time together?

I want to challenge you this week to pray and ask God what the best way is to communicate with your children. Then make some time that week to do what God says to do.

1. **Are you communicating effectively with your children? If not, why?**
2. **Ask God to show you what your children need to communicate?**
3. **Design a plan to help them develop their weakness.**
4. **Ask your children the best way to communicate with them.**

98

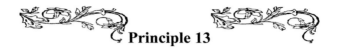

Principle 13

SIMPLICITY

"And to make it your ambition to lead a quite life and attend to your own business and work with your hands, just as we commanded you."
1Thesssalonians 4:11

I've heard it said that the simple things in life produce the greatest pleasures. It took me becoming a single mother to genuinely understand the meaning of that phrase. My life changed dramatically after becoming a single mom. There was neither the time nor the finances to do all the things that I used to do.

I am so grateful for this new time in my life. I discovered that spending time with my son, and doing everyday things together was better than any theme park could offer. The time we spend together has brought us closer together. It has also been one of the greatest teaching tools I have to teach my son the practical, everyday things of life. He needs to know these things when he is on his own, and gets married. (I want a happy daughter in law!)

There are three words that describe a single mom's life; do, do and do. It seems life does not stop for a mere second with all that we are responsible for on our own. It is extremely easy to forget what is truly valuable in life; the blessing of our children. We must learn as single moms the people in our house are more important than the actual place. Do not get caught up in all the chores, cooking, cleaning, laundry and places you have to go, and fail to devote the time necessary with your children.

I know a single mom with two children that is a real neat freak. From the moment she gets up, until she goes to bed she is "doing" something around the house. She is constantly vacuuming, wiping floors and counters, sweeping, dusting or cleaning out the car. Now that is not a terrible thing, and God does require excellence in our home. What is wrong is that she puts the "doing" around her home as more important than the "being" with the children in her home.

We tend to make things harder on ourselves than they truly are as single moms. It is possible to live a quiet, simple life as 1Thesssalonians 4:11 instructs us to do, **"And to make it your ambition to lead a quite life and attend to your own business and work with your hands, just as we commanded you."** We must learn to keep things uncomplicated in life, and keep our homes as calm and peaceful as possible.

In this Principle of Simplicity, I will to teach you the "KISS" system which stands for **Keep It Simple Single Mom.** Keep everything that you do as effortless as possible. Simplicity allows you more time with your children, and saves time and money. Most important though, simplicity reserves your sanity. Below are three areas that help me keep mine.

1. Simple Housework.

Having the weekend free to spend time with my son is extremely important to me. I do not want to spend all day on Saturday cleaning the house. It is also important to me to honor God on the Sabbath. In order to accomplish this, we clean the house a little bit every day. We break our chores up into "bite sized" pieces.

There is nothing better for me than to play with my son. Eric loves to race and always tries to beat his record. I know that my son's communication style is playing, so I turned our chores into a race. We set a time frame to get the job done, and turn the dreaded house cleaning into

"Beat the clock." This worked when he was much younger and still now as a teenager. I was able to accomplish several goals working like this:

1. I was able to spend time with my son.
2. I was able to reach out to him with his own communication style.
3. The house got cleaned, and we did it together.
4. Eric learned how to clean a house which will help him in the future.
5. I achieved a personal goal to have the weekend free.

We made a list of all the tasks required to clean the house. Then we chose the jobs we liked to do, and played rock, paper, scissors for the remaining ones. We set a goal to accomplish each chore in a fifteen minute time frame. Here is what our weekly schedule looks like.

Monday: Sweep and mop the floors, laundry, dishes and kitchen.
Tuesday: Dust and vacuum, dishes and kitchen.
Wednesday: Clean Eric's and guest bathroom, dishes and kitchen.
Thursday: Clean my bathroom, laundry, dishes and kitchen.
Friday: Garbage, yard, dishes and kitchen.
Saturday: Dishes and kitchen.
Sunday: Dishes and kitchen.

I know heavier cleaning needs to be done that requires more time. Following this simple, straightforward process will get the basics done while spending time with your children.

2. Simple Meals

The Lord laid on my heart for us single moms to *stop eating fast food,* and make nutritious home cooked meals. Most fast food is inherently unhealthy any how. Our children need to smell the aromas of food cooking in our house. This creates warmth in a home, and makes memories for them that will last a lifetime.

A single mom's best friends in the kitchen are a crock pot, casserole dishes and freezer bags. If you do not have a crock pot make a fifteen dollar investment in one, or ask for one as a gift. It will be worth thousands of dollars saved in time and money in the long run. A casserole dish with a cover is about four dollars, and a box of freezer bags is about one dollar and fifty cents.

You can make a delicious meal in the crock pot the night before or early in the morning. All that is left to do is turn it on, and let it slowly simmer through out the day. Your family will come home to an enjoyable, hot, home cooked meal. This leaves time to spend with your children when you get home from a long hard day at work. You do not have to worry about cooking dinner the minute you walk thru the door. There is nothing sweeter to my ears than when Eric walks in the door and just stops to take in the smells of the feast that is cooking. I just love it when he says, "Mom, what smells so good? What are we having for dinner?"

My son takes his lunch to school from the meals I cook at home. This offers him warm, healthy food to eat instead of wasting money on unhealthy school lunches. His friends are exceptionally jealous that he has home cooked meals. Many of them say they wish their mom cooked like that, and they're moms are married! (How impressive are you single mom?)

They're also frozen meals in your grocery store just for the crock pot. All you do is put the bag of meat and vegetables in the crock pot and add water. The prices are exceptionally reasonable also. You can astonishingly feed a family of five for around five dollars. Pay close attention to the fat and sodium content in some of these meals. You do not want to sacrifice health for something cheap and easy.

Another form of wonderfully delicious, easy meals is one dish casseroles. Organize your meal plan for the week, and put the casseroles together as a family. Just pop it in the oven when you get home from work, and you have a lovely, affordable home cooked meal.   Recipes are available online for crock pot meals, casseroles or one -dish meals, and they are free. This is something terrific you can do in a 21Principles small group also. Plan some meals together then each person can bring certain ingredients and a casserole dish. Together you can construct a meal or two and have dishes ready for the week.

The barbecue is another excellent tool I love to use. I grill several varieties and batches of meat. After they cool, I wrap them up and freeze them. All that is left to do is take out what you need the night before and let it thaw in the refrigerator. When you get home from work, simply put it in the microwave to heat. It truly tastes like it just came off the grill. Make some easy side dishes, and you have a magnificent home cooked meal.   When cooking, make a double batch of meals, and freeze them for quick, easy, already prepared meals in the future. All you have to do is cook a healthy side dish and some steamed vegetables. Then simply add some fruit and you are ready to eat.

These few ideas create fabulous home cooked meals, and save a lot of money. Fast food is expensive, generally fattening and offers you almost no nutritional value. Cooking at home provides proper nutrition, and glorious memories that last a lifetime. Turning a simple crock pot meal into an elaborate showing is easy, and will make meal time memorable. My son and I adore eating by candle light and listening to classical music. With just some simple, basic things you can make a dramatic presentation.

For example, a set table says "welcome home" to our children. Take a few extra minutes before you go to bed and set your table for breakfast the next day. After breakfast or before you leave for work in the morning, set the table for dinner. This is also fun to do as a family when you get home. It is amazing how willing the children are to help with the delicious aroma of dinner cooking in the crock pot. Put on a table cloth or place mats. I loved using some of the things Eric made in school as a center piece. It made for enjoyable conversation about his day. Just a single rose or a few flowers can change the entire mood of a wild, crazy day, and only costs pennies to do. Just some basic things can make your children feel enormously special. This creates an atmosphere that will make everyone want to come together to talk and be a family. Again, these are memories that our children will treasure for a lifetime, and so will you.

3. Simple Fun.

There are so many simple things we can do with our children that bring joy and happiness. For so long, I felt ashamed that I could not afford to take my son to places like Disney Land or go on great vacations.

In the long run though, all our children truly want is for us to spend time with them. Some of my best memories from my own childhood are playing board games with my family on Sunday nights. Spend a little money and *invest* in some board games and cards. They are inexpensive, and a terrific way to meet around the table and have fun together. Invite some friends over and make a night out of it. Children love to be outside playing ball, so go out and play with them. It does not matter if you can throw or not, just go out and be with them. Your time is all they are genuinely looking for.

Instead of going out to a restaurant for dinner, make a picnic either indoors, or outdoors. I found a small indoor s'mores maker for only a couple of dollars at a garage sale. We camp indoors and make this our "bon fire." Riding bikes or playing tennis is a terrific, simple way to exercise and be together. Of course there is nothing like snuggling on the couch and watching a great movie. They are available now in stores to rent for only one dollar.

It works best to ask your children what they want to play and just do it with them. You will be amazed at the simplicity of children. Remember, all they honestly want is you. The main thing is to keep the priorities straight; life is about the people first and then the place. Simplicity is something that is free, and keeping things easy brings true peace.

1. **List the chores needed to be done. Break them into "Bite Size" pieces, and assign a family member to each of them.**
2. **List five simple meals you can cook for the week.**
3. **How can you make the atmosphere of meal time memorable?**
4. **List several simple things you can do for family entertainment.**

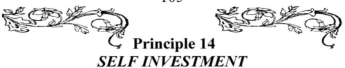

Principle 14
SELF INVESTMENT

"Be of sober spirit, be on the alert. Your adversary, the devil, prowls around like a roaring lion, seeking someone to devour." 1Peter 5:8-8

I had time on my hands when I became a single mom that I did not know what to do with. It was the time after my son went to bed that I struggled with the most. The house was extremely quiet, and with no one to talk to I was terribly lonely. All I did was drown my sorrows in front of the TV watching stupid shows. I also got fat from eating away my agony with junk food. If I was not doing that, I was entertaining Satan with my tea parties of self pity. All I did was think about how awful this single mom life was.

The Lord spoke to me about this one night after I put Eric to bed. He told me to devote the next six months of my life to only reading at night. I needed to spend time at the Christian bookstore and get some books, then lock myself in at night and read them. I had been to a Christian bookstore only once before, and that was to get my Bible. I had absolutely no concept of what I should read. The next day I prayed as I walked through the doors of the bookstore. I asked God to lead me to exactly what He wanted me to read. The women's section seemed like the most logical place to start. I stood in front of the wall of books and prayed, "God show me what you want me read." All of a sudden, it seemed like two books literally jumped off of the shelves at me. The first one was "Loving God with All Your Mind," by Elizabeth George. The other one was "What to do until Love Finds You," by Michelle McKinney Hammond. I highly suggest that you read both of them.

I did what God said to do and started to read. Every second of extra time I had was devoted to reading my Bible first, and then these books next. I was so fascinated by them I could not stop reading. They got to know me extremely well at the bookstore. For the next six months I read, and read, and I have not stopped since. There is no time to be lonely or have pity parties. My personal library is now my most treasured earthy possession after my pictures of Eric.

All of the wasted time I spent in front of the TV or wallowing was nothing more than an open door to the enemy. The Bible says in 1Peter 5:8, **"Be of sober spirit, be on the alert. Your adversary, the devil, prowls around like a roaring lion, seeking someone to devour."** God tells us how to avoid the enemy in the beginning of verse 9, **"But resist him, and be firm in your faith."**

I am extremely passionate about this Principle because I believe single moms are the enemy's number one prime target. What does it say in verse eight that the enemy does? He prowls around like a roaring lion seeking someone to devour. What manner of food do you think a hungry roaring lion looks for in the jungle? If you have ever watched any of the animal shows on TV that demonstrate a lion chasing after prey, they pursue weak, young or straggling animals. They want prey who are isolated and not on the alert. That is exactly what I was like in being a new single mom; weak spiritually, emotionally, mentally and physically and I was all alone. That is exactly where Satan wants you and does his best work.

Look at what Peter says to do in the beginning of verse eight; **"Be sober, be alert."** This is a notification to watch out for Satan, especially during times of adversity. A healthy single mom keeps her mind and body alert at all times. You cannot fill your mind with trashy TV shows, romance novels, or your own troubles and expect to be victorious.

Peter says in verse nine to **"resist Satan and be firm in your faith."** That means to expand your mind with the things of God, and not the world's garbage. I think the reason God wanted me to read at night is that I was dangerous to myself and my son. I was young in my faith, and weak as a single mom. I was an obvious target for the enemy. I watched stupid TV programs, read romance novels trying to heal my broken heart, and looked for love in all the wrong places.

The Bible says in Proverbs 15:4, **"The heart of him who has understanding seeks knowledge, but the mouth of fool's feeds on foolishness."** Thank goodness God cared enough about me, and my son to send me to the Christian bookstore. He cares about you and your children to and I believe He is asking you to do the same thing.

I learned to use my time more constructively from Elizabeth George's Book, "A Woman After Gods Own Heart," by creating five "Fat files." Get five different colored files, and then select five areas that you wish to become an expert in about the things of God. Remember what Proverbs 15:4 said about those who seek knowledge? Make sure that your five areas have eternal rewards.

If you are not sure what areas you would choose to be an expert in, review your life plan. Search through the things pertinent about life to you, and then explore your bible to find information about these areas. Elizabeth did a real neat thing with her fat files and Bible. Each file was color coded, so when she studied her bible she would highlight the verses that stood out to her that related to one of her topics in that color. Along with five files, you would also need five different colored highlighters. One of the areas I wanted to be an expert in is the Proverbs 31 Woman. I just love her, and I want to spend the rest of my life trying to model her. I bought a binder with numerical tabs in it from 1-21 to cover Proverbs 31 verses 10-31. I have this with me every time that I read my Bible or other books. If I find something that relates to one of the twenty one verses, I write it down in that section. Before I knew it, I had a wealth of information in there. I also wanted to learn about how to be a successful, godly single woman in this world. I studied some of the foremost women that were, or still are single such as; Elizabeth Elliott, Amy Carmichael and Michelle McKinney Hammond to name a few. They inspired and motivated me by the lives they led for God.

Who knows what will happen from all of the information you gather? Someday you might write a book out of it, or a Bible Study series to share with other people.

My former employer, Dr. John Maxwell is an expert on leadership. He started a file like this on leadership when he was just a young man. If he read something about leadership, he would make a copy of it and tuck it away in his file. When he decided to write his first book he had a wealth of information already on hand. Now he is known around the world for his expertise on leadership. Here is a powerful tip: When you begin to feel lonely or depressed, take out one of your five fat files and begin to work on it. Use your mind for God's work and get out of yourself.

You may be thinking, "I am not meant to be known around the world." Maybe you are or maybe you are not. What is essential is that you develop your mind with the things of God. It is up to him what doors he will open for you to share that knowledge with others. When I first went to the bookstore, I never dreamed I would be doing something like this.

It all starts with being obedient. If the Lord has laid something on your heart to do, your business is to get it done. God knows what the next step is for you with this project. He can not do anything with it though until it is finished. I wasted so much of God's time thinking that I was not worthy to do anything like this. I constantly tried to figure out how God would use all of the information I had accumulated. These are not the right variety of things to be thinking about. Our only job is to start where God asks us to. He will open the next door when you are finished.

Pretend for a moment you were asked to teach a class on one of your fat files. Would you be ready to do so? The Bible says in 2 Timothy 4:2, **"Be prepared in season and out."** Create a summary of what you would want some one to know about your subject. Then it is a matter of filling in the information.

The point of the verse in 2 Timothy 4:2 is to make your self prepared to teach. You might remember in the "Principle of Influence," that I taught my son everything I knew first. That was a perfect place to plant a first seed into. In due time, God took the work that I did, which I thought was just for me personally, and turned it into something professional.

I have been able to leave the corporate world and stay at home with my son to fulfill my passion and purpose in life. Who knows how God may reward you financially for the work you have done? You might just be asked to talk about your topic someday, and receive a blessing for it.

I was extremely passionate about sharing these Principles with other women. I went to churches and practically begged them to let me come in and teach their single moms for free. I did that for a couple of years before a church finally called me. They invited me to speak at a dinner for their single moms, and they paid me for it. Now it is what I do full time along with sell my 21Principles Bible Study and book. It was out of that "readiness" that God allowed me to do this. All I did was create an outline, and then fill it in with what I wanted single moms to know. I made myself available to God to use me, and left the rest up to him.

We need to teach our children marvelous things that they will carry with them for the rest of their lives. We also need to be an example of a Godly woman and mother. Our daughters may look to us and want to model their lives after us. Our sons may look to our example when they choose a wife someday. Please consider what you want your children to see in you as an example of a woman and mother.

Consider applying these five areas to your life this week and then implement them into a life- long strategy.

Turn off the television. (Except for the news. You need to stay informed about the world) Make a commitment to use your time wisely for God, yourself and your children.

Be determined to expand your mind with the things of God. Throw out all the trashy books and magazines you may have in your house, and restore your library based off of God's truth.

Get five folders and different colored markers. Determine what you want your areas of expertise to be. It is alright if you can not come up with five right now. The point is to at least start even if you only have one. By faith, purchase the five folders so you are "prepared in season and out."

Commit to preparation. Read some books and attend seminars or classes about your particular spheres of expertise you chose.

Commit to completion. Make a goal to "be prepared." Set a date that you will be ready to teach one of your subjects. Once your project is finished, commit your availability to God. Watch how He will open doors for you to help others.

 I know that you are going to do great at this, and I look forward to reading your material that will come out of this.

1. In what ways are you using your time that does not glorify God?
2. How can you use your time to fill your mind with the things of God?
3. List several things you would like to become an expert in?
4. What can you do on a daily basis to start investing in your self?

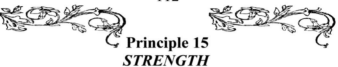

Principle 15
STRENGTH

"She sets about her work vigorously; her arms are strong for her tasks". Proverbs 31:17

I used food as a means to relieve pain and rejection. Other women do the opposite with bulimia and anorexia. I thought if my body looked terrific, I would be loved and accepted by men and other influential people in my life. I was constantly on a diet or participating in the latest diet craze. Unfortunately, this started for me at an exceptionally young age. Over the years I have developed extremely unhealthy eating habits, and completely disrespected the body God gave me.

At one time I was a lovely size eight. I was healthy on the outside, but messed up on the inside from all the strongholds I was dealing with. (See Principle 3) Now, I am better than ever on the inside and somewhat out of balance on the outside. I am, however, working my way back to the size eight with proper nutrition and exercise.

I somehow misinterpreted what Paul meant in the Bible when he said that we are to "buffet our bodies." It took me a while to realize he did not mean the all you can eat food bar. He meant that we are to control our bodies and appetite; not let them control us.

It is imperative as single moms, that our physical bodies are healthy and strong. We need an enormous amount of energy to keep up with everything on our plate. (No pun intended) Our physical body is also the precise dwelling place of God. The Bible says in 1 Corinthians 6:19-20, **"Or do you not know that your body is the temple of the**

Holy Spirit who is in you, whom you have from God, and that you are not your own? For you were bought at a price; therefore glorify God in your body and in your spirit, which are Gods."

In the past, I never once considered that this body I have is not my own. I ate to mask pain and stuffed things like chocolate, ice cream, chips, sodas, junk food and sweets into my mouth. Our body is the physical casing for the Holy Spirit, and we need to take proper care of it. I represent God as his word says in Romans 12:1, **"I beseech you therefore, brethren, by the mercies of God, that you present your bodies a living sacrifice holy, acceptable to God, which is your reasonable service."**

Our body is the mechanism we use to do the things which God has purposed for us. If we fail to take proper care of it, we suppress the Holy Spirit from working through us to the fullest extent. There is nothing on this earth worth eating to thwart the Holy Spirit of God working through me. We need to take seriously what 1Cornithians 10:31 says, **"Therefore, whether you eat or drink or whatever you do, do all to the glory of God."**

I desperately needed help in the area of proper nutrition, and once again I cried out to God for the answer. The Lord simply said, *"If I didn't make it, don't eat it."* Buffeting, or disciplining our body, means to analyze everything we put into our mouth. Now, when I have an urge to eat something God did not make, I weigh eating it against the Holy Spirit working in me.

My weakness is sweets and I absolutely adore carrot cake with double cream cheese frosting. Unfortunately, there is a store right around the corner from me that makes the best carrot cake I have ever had. When I drive past that store, my car literally turns into the parking lot on its own. I have actually sat in that parking lot listening to the enemy say, "That carrot cake sure would taste good right now. Go ahead and eat it. You have worked hard today. You deserve it." I literally sit in the car weighing whether to go buy carrot cake, or have the Holy Spirit working in me to the fullest. When you look at it from that perspective, the carrot cake does not seem particularly appealing after all. A better choice would be some nice, fresh carrots that God made.

I wonder what Jesus would eat if he were here in the flesh right now? If we are here to enforce God's word here on earth, why not eat only the foods listed in the Bible? As soon as I thought about this I heard the enemy whisper, "Jesus did not have carrot cake, chips, french fries, chocolate, doughnuts and all of the delicious things that you can have here now." That is true, but the real question is, "Do you think Jesus would eat those things if he had the choice?" I believe God in the flesh would not fill his temple with sugars, processed or fast foods and other downright junk. Possibly a better question to ask is what would we feed Jesus if he were here in the flesh today?

I researched the Bible to see what foods God made to now use as my own food plan. Below are the foods of the basic food groups; grains, fruits, vegetables, dairy and meat found in the Bible.

GRAINS
There is a fabulous Biblical bread right in our grocery freezer today called Ezekiel Bread. It is made from the exact same ingredients the Lord told Ezekiel to make his bread with in Ezekiel 4:9 which are wheat, barley, beans, lentils, millet, rye legumes and beans. Other grains listen in the Bible include: Barley (Deuteronomy 8:8; Ezekiel

4:9) Bread (Genesis 25:34; 2 Samuel 6:19; 16:1; Mark 8:14) Corn (Matthew 12:1; KJV - refers to "grain" such as wheat or barley) Flour (2 Samuel 17:28; 1 Kings 17:12) Millet (Ezekiel 4:9) Spelt (Ezekiel 4:9) Unleavened Bread (Genesis 19:3; Exodus 12:20) Wheat (Ezra 6:9; Deuteronomy 8:8) These grains provide a powerful source of fiber and help prevent infections, constipation, hemorrhoids, varicose veins. They also protect against colon cancer. I read an impressive line about any form of white bread that said, "The whiter the bread, the sooner you are dead." Make sure when you go to select breads, pastas or snacks, that the labels read whole wheat or whole grain.

FRUITS
Fruits are most likely what Jesus would have eaten with a meal of fish, bread and vegetables. Fruits make a perfect snack or dessert especially when topped with honey and nuts. The fruits and nuts mentioned in the Bible are; Apples (Song of Solomon 2:5), Almonds (Genesis 43:11; Numbers 17:8) Dates (2 Samuel 6:19; 1 Chronicles 16:3), Figs (Nehemiah 13:15; Jeremiah 24:1-3), Grapes (Leviticus 19:10; Deuteronomy 23:24), Melons (Numbers 11:5; Isaiah 1:8), Olives (Isaiah 17:6; Micah 6:15), Pistachio Nuts (Genesis 43:11), Pomegranates (Numbers 20:5; Deuteronomy 8:8), Raisins (Numbers 6:3; 2 Samuel 6:19) and Sycamore Fruit (Psalm 78:47; Amos 7:14)

VEGTABLES
It seems that manna from heaven could not change the pleasure of fresh vegetables as stated in Numbers 11:5 6, "We remember the fish, which we did eat in Egypt freely; the cucumbers, and the melons, and the leeks, and the melons, and the garlic. But now our soul is dried away: there is nothing at all, beside the manna, before our eyes." Vegetables can be eaten raw or frozen, and you can fix

them by steaming or lightly stir frying them in olive oil.
They also make a succulent one dish meal mixed with
spices, beans or brown rice. Other vegetables listed in the
bible are; Beans (2 Samuel 17:28; Ezekiel 4:9),
Cucumbers (Numbers 11:5), Gourds (2 Kings 4:39), Leeks
(Numbers 11:5), Lentils (Genesis 25:34; Ezekiel 4:9) and
Onions (Numbers 11:5). Beans, peas, and lentils are a
fantastic source of protein and provide our body with
vitamin c and act as antioxidants. These beans include
garbanzo beans or chick peas, lima beans, green peas, black
eyed peas, white beans, navy beans, black beans and kidney
beans.

DAIRY

The Hebrews made butter from milk (Proverbs 30: 33), and
something called leben; a runny yogurt prepared in leather
bags from the milk of goats or camels. Curds were also
popular dairy foods. (2 Samuel 17: 29; 1 Samuel 17: 18;
and Job 10:10). Other forms of dairy products listed in the
Bible are; Butter (Proverbs 30:33), Milk (Exodus 33:3; Job
10:10; Judges 5:25) and Eggs (Job 6:6; Luke 11:12)

MEAT

Jesus' diet included mainly bread and fish. Beef was
usually reserved for feasts or receptions. The best quality of
fish to eat is clean fish with fins and scales from the waters
of Alaska, Mexico, South America, New Zealand and
Iceland. The waters are exceptionally pure around these
areas. Avoid eating seafood that resides near the bottom of
water. God designed them to be cleansing agents to collect
toxic waste, viruses, parasites and bacteria. These would
include catfish, clams, oysters, shrimp, prawns, scallops,
crabs and lobsters. Animal meats listed in the Bible
include Calf (Proverbs 15:17; Luke 15:23), Goat (Genesis

27:9), Lamb (2 Samuel 12:4), Oxen (1 Kings 19:21), Sheep (Deuteronomy 14:4)Venison (Genesis 27:7 <u>KJV</u>) and Fowl include: Dove (Leviticus 12:8), Pigeon (Genesis 15:9; Leviticus 12:8), Quail (Psalm 105:40) and Partridge (1 Samuel 26:20; Jeremiah 17:11)
Another exceptionally healthy form of protein is soy. This can easily and inexpensively replace meat in various forms. Soy is also free of hormones and steroids.

SEASONING AND SPICES
These are fabulous to have for cooking for they add such marvelous flavors to our food. Ones listed in the Bible include; Salt (Ezra 6:9; Job 6:6), Rue (Luke 11:42), Mustard (Matthew 13:31), Mint (Matthew 23:23; Luke 11:42), Garlic (Numbers 11:5), Dill (Matthew 23:23), Cumin (Isaiah 28:25; Matthew 23:23), Cinnamon (Exodus 30:23; Revelation 18:13), Coriander (Exodus 16:31; Numbers 11:7), Anise (Matthew 23:23 <u>KJV</u>).

MISCELLANEOUS ITEMS
These wonderful foods are staples in our kitchens, and ones we use often such as; Wine (Ezra 6:9; John 2:1-10) only for cooking of course, Vinegar (Ruth 2:14; John 19:29), Olive Oil (Ezra 6:9; Deuteronomy 8:8), Honey (Exodus 33:3; Deuteronomy 8:8; Judges 14:8-9) and Grape Juice (Numbers 6:3)

Water is the most essential nutrient for your body. Two thirds of your body weight is water, and it is vital for carrying nutrients to the cells of your body. You also need enough water in your body to release and eliminate waste products. It is crucial to drink at least one gallon of water a day.

To gain the strength we need as single moms it is vital to exercise several times a week. Some of the physical benefits of exercise are prevention of heart disease, diabetes, high blood pressure, colon cancer, depression and anxiety. Exercise helps control your weight and builds healthy bones, muscles and joints. It also helps us psychologically by releasing brain chemicals such as serotonin, dopamine, norepinephrine and endorphins. This helps reduce stress, anxiety and depression. Exercise strengthens the immune system and gives us more energy. It also helps us look better and develop a stronger self image.

What form of exercise did Jesus do? He did not have the benefit of health clubs, exercise videos and sports that we do now. He did do something that every single mom can do, and that is walk. Jesus walked everywhere. Did you know that walking is the most effective way to shape up your gluteus, develop toned calves and get slimmer thighs? Best of all, walking does not cost anything, and it is easy to do. Speed walking burns almost as many calories as jogging –without damaging your joints.

Practice proper form by walking tall, relax your shoulders and turn your elbows 90 degrees. Land on your heel and roll through your foot, pushing off firmly with your toes for maximum calf toning. Alternate speeds when you walk by starting slow and then increase your pace. Walk at a speed where it is difficult to hold a conversation. The longer you stay at this pace, the harder your muscles will work, and the more calories you will burn. Walk uphill to burn more calories and tone the derriere. (I read this is what Jennifer Lopez does, and we all know how good she looks) This is a terrific exercise you can do with your children also. I power walk with my dogs and Eric rides his bike along side of me. You can also walk with your neighbors and friends for the companionship and encouragement.

Exercising is so advantageous for releasing toxins in your body; it improves circulation and repairs and rejuvenates your skin along with many other things. Make it a point to do something at least four to five times a week. As the phrase goes, "Just do it." Exercise for you and your children should be a non-negotiable in your daily routine whether you feel like doing it or not.

What I genuinely want to accomplish in this Principle is to teach you how to eat right and exercise for all of the right reasons listed below.

1. This is what Jesus did.

2. Eating right and exercising gives glory to Gods temple.

3. It will give us the strength to accomplish everything that we have to do.

4. It will extend our lives so we have more time to serve God, and be with our children.

It is absolutely praiseworthy to look terrific and present your self well in a nice dress or that perfect pair of blue jeans. The point of this Principle is to make sure that is not your first priority. Our true desire should be to take proper care of God's temple. It is the temple of the Holy Spirit, and our appearance represents Christ to our families and others.

1. **What changes do you need to make in your daily eating habits to eat only what God made?**
2. **Implement a plan to include exercise each day for your self and your children.**

Notes: What Would Jesus Eat? Don Colbert, MD; Foods of the Bible, Mary Fairchild, About.com Guide

PART THREE

BALANCE
AND
HARMONY

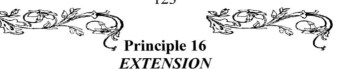

Principle 16
EXTENSION

"And if you give yourself to the hungry and satisfy the desire of the afflicted, then your light will rise in the darkness and your gloom will become like the midday."

Isaiah 58:10

My life changed dramatically from a desperate, depressed, lonely, selfish, single mom to one of fulfillment by learning a paradoxical spiritual principle. This Principle was formed when a remarkable woman, by the name of Jill Briscoe, signed one of her books for me. She wrote the verse from Isaiah 58:11 that said, **"The Lord will guide you always. He will satisfy your needs in a sun scorched land and strengthen your frame. You will become like a well watered garden, like a spring whose waters never fail."**

I will never forget what I did when I read that verse for the first time; I laughed! I said to my self, "Right! Me like a well watered garden, like a spring whose waters never fail? Not with the way I feel right now. I feel horrible about myself, and this single mom life." For the next two weeks though, I could not get that verse out of my mind. It wore on me that God had so much more for me than the way I was living it; depressed and lonely as a single mother.

The thoughts in my head of that verse were just beautiful. I pictured the bright colors of the flowers, and I could smell their sweet fragrance. I imagined scooping up some of the deep, rich, dark earth and letting it sift through my fingers. I also pictured a babbling brook in this spectacular garden. I could feel the spray from the cool water as it tumbled over the rocks. This picture of a "well watered garden" was a far cry from my dry, desert land of single motherhood.

After two weeks of thinking about Isaiah 58:11 over and over, I finally asked God to teach me how to become like a well watered garden, like a spring whose waters never fail. As always, the Lord answered me and simply said, *"Look at the verse ahead of that."* It said, **"And if you give yourself to the hungry and satisfy the desire of the afflicted, then your light will rise in the darkness and your gloom will become like the midday."**

Life is not meant to be lived in sorrow, and isolation thinking only of myself and my problems. In her book, "Let me be a Woman," Elizabeth Elliott beautifully describes this paradoxical principle of Isaiah 58:10. She so eloquently said, "You yourself will be given light in exchange for pouring yourself out for the hungry; you yourself will get guidance, the satisfaction of your longings, and strength, when you pour yourself out, when you make the satisfaction of somebody else's desire your own concern; you yourself will be a source of refreshment, a builder, a leader into healing and rest at a time when things around you seem to have crumbled."

If I wanted to have real joy in my life I had to get out of myself, and get into others. Nowhere in the Bible does it say that life is all about me. Satan wants you isolated, depressed and focused just on yourself. The Bible says in Philippians 2:3-5, **"Do nothing from selfishness or empty conceit, but with humility of mind regard one another as more important than yourself; do not merely look out for your own personal interests, but also for the interests of others. Have this attitude in yourselves which was also in Christ Jesus."**

If our purpose in life is to become Christ like and conform to His character, then we need to do what Jesus did. He knew that he was going to the cross to die. I can not find anywhere in my Bible where it says that he sat around lonely and depressed with a "woe is me" perspective focusing just on himself. I can not find anywhere where Jesus said, "Oh God, why did this have to happen to me?" The verse in Philippians 2:7 says, **"He emptied himself, taking the form of a bond-servant."** In other words, Jesus lived to serve others which is what we should be doing as healthy single mothers. In doing this pure joy will come to you.

I love the analogy comparing the Sea of Galilee and the Dead Sea. The Sea of Galilee is a lake full of life because it takes in water but also gives it out. In contrast, nothing lives in the Dead Sea because there is no outflow, so everything in it is stagnated.

It is very selfish to continually dwell on my own problems and myself. How could I possibly notice anyone else, and what they might be struggling with if all I thought about was my self? Once I understood this paradoxical spiritual principle I went from asking, "What about me? To whose need's can I meet today?

The Bible says in Ephesians 2:10, **"For we are His workmanship, created in Christ Jesus for good works, which God prepared beforehand so that we could walk in them."** God has a plan for your life, and it is called your ministry or service. Life here on earth is about eternity. One day we will stand before God, and He will ask us "What on earth were you doing for me?" The only answer I could give God as a single mother would be "absolutely nothing." The truth is that all I thought about was me. Oh, I had a lot of excuses to use as a single mom. I was too busy, or there is not enough time to take care of my own family, let alone help someone else out." I do not believe God is going to accept those excuses when we stand before Him. We lose our eternal rewards by being so selfish here on earth.

We all have a ministry of some form, and our ministry is everywhere we go. Yes, we are busy as single mothers, but we still have to go the grocery store and run errands. Have you ever met a cashier having a lousy day or that could not wait to go home? Then have the nerve to tell you all about it as you are paying your hard earned money to them? This is not the attitude I want to see when I give my money to someone. I want them to serve me! God says to serve them though. You could give them a compliment or say something to brighten their day. Do you drive somewhere in your car as a single mom? How many times have you faced a "driving maniac" that cut you off? Instead of preventing them from getting ahead of you, let them in and say a prayer for them. Do you work at a job or are you around other people? I promise that someone around you is hurting even more than you are. It is ministry when you offer them a shoulder to cry on or perhaps a smile. Ask God to put someone in your path today that you can help. Then ask him for the courage you need to actually do it.

I was in sales when I became a single mom, so I was able to work out of my house a fair amount of time. One day I was relishing being able to work in the peace and quiet of my home. Right after I started to work I heard the Lord say, "Go to the office." All I could say back to him was, "Lord, I do not want to go to the office. I have a deadline on this project, and I am way behind. I'll never get this work done there with all of the distractions." As I continued on with my work, and my selfish outlook, the Lord kept nudging gently at my spirit to go to the office. I could not handle it anymore, so I packed up my things and headed to the office. I was quite angry at God because I had a large amount of work to do. As soon as I got to my desk, one of my co-workers come over to me in tears. She said she was so glad to me. She had been praying all morning that I would come in, even though I was scheduled to be out that day. Something terrible was happening in her life, and she asked me if I would pray with her about this situation.

I also remember the times that I have blown it when God put someone in my path to help. One day my son had a terrible stomach ache, and he was not feeling well. He wanted a milk shake, so I went through a drive thru restaurant and ordered one. As I drove up to the window to pay I heard the Lord say, *"Tell the young man at the window that I love him very much."* I genuinely wanted to tell him, but all I could think of was Eric not feeling well. I had my own problems too, so I did not do it. My son gets extremely embarrassed whenever I do things like that, and I was not in the mood to deal with him either.

I knew better than that. I know that I need to do what God says to do when he says to do it, and not worry about the rest. There are serious consequences of not obeying God when He tells you to help someone.

I still think about that young man and wonder if that small message from God could have changed his life. It still haunts me that I did not do what the Lord asked of me. I had no inkling what he was going through. What if that one message from God could have turned his life around that day? God knows what is going on in the lives of his children, and he knows exactly what they need and when they need it. God knew that young man needed to hear that He loved him, and he was counting on me to tell him. What if that young man was thinking about committing suicide that day? What if he was not a believer and got killed that day? God gave me that responsibility to tell someone else about his love, and all I could think about was my self. I did not know what serving others truly meant when I became a Christian. I thought it meant that you had to be "called" into the ministry in order to serve, such as becoming a Pastor or a missionary. God calls us into service when we welcome him as our Lord and Savior. Anytime you use your God given abilities to help others, you are fulfilling your calling.

Maybe you are wondering, "What is my calling?" Go back to your life plan and take a look at the things that are important about life to you, or your five fat files of things you want to be an expert in. Something in there just might be your "calling."

God gave me these "21 Principles of a Healthy Single Mom," and my own story to put with them. I believe they are a part of my "calling." God will use the painful experiences we have been through to minister to others. I have discovered through my time as a single mom that my greatest ministry has come out of my deepest sorrow and anguish.

The bible says is 2 Corinthians 1:4, **"Who comforts us in all our affliction so that we will be able to comfort those who are in any affliction with the comfort with which we ourselves are comforted by God."** The more we suffer, the more God comforts us. Every trial that you encounter will help you comfort other people who are suffering similar troubles. Nothing has been more satisfying to me than to share what God taught me in my worst of times when I became a single mom. Rick Warren puts it all together in his book, "The Purpose Driven Life" when he says, "The very experiences that you have resented or regretted most in life – the ones you've wanted to hide and forget – are the experiences God wants to use to help others. They are your ministry!"

For God to use your painful experiences you must be willing to share them. You have to stop covering them up, and you must honestly admit your faults, failures, and fears. This will be your most powerful instrument of ministry.

People are always encouraged when we share how God's grace helped us in our weakness, rather than brag about our strengths.

God's ways are not our ways, and something supernatural happens when we get out of ourselves and pour into others. When we reach out to other people and do what God says to do, when He says to do it, he will make sure all of our needs are supplied. When you focus on being a blessing to others, God will make sure that you are blessed in abundance.

A woman in my church complimented me several times on a necklace I had. As I was driving to work one morning, the Lord told me to send it to her. I have to admit I did not know why he would want me to give up my necklace. I was not thrilled about it for it was the only necklace I had. I was obedient though and sent it to her in the mail with a note of encouragement.

A couple of days later she called me in tears thanking me for it. She told me that she was going through an extremely difficult time, and that she needed a touch from the Lord. That necklace showed her how much God cared for her. After I heard those words, I could have cared less about not having that necklace any more. My heart was filled with joy that I obeyed God and made someone else happy.

About a week later, I received a check from someone at church for two hundred dollars. She simply wanted me to know how much she appreciated my ministry. Along with the check, she gave me detailed instructions to get some things that I need just for myself, such as clothes and jewelry. When God blesses, he blesses in abundance. The necklace that I gave away was only worth twenty dollars. Because of my obedience God blessed it a hundred times over.

When I first made the decision to "get out of myself," I asked God to put someone in my path that I could help. I did not have to go any farther than right outside of my own front door. My next door neighbor was going through a divorce from a marriage of twenty five years. All I had to give her was my shoulder to cry on, and tell her that I understood. As we talked a little more, I was able to reach out to her and share some of the things that God had been teaching me. We developed an exceptionally deep friendship and have been close friends for several years now. That my dear single mom is what having a calling and serving is all about!

If you honestly want to flourish as a single mother, you have to learn to give instead of receive. The bible says in Galatians 6:7, **"Do not be deceived, God is not mocked; for whatever a man sows this he will also reap."** All I ever wanted to do was help other single moms get healed. In wanting to help others, I think I received the most healing. Every time the Lord allows me to speak and share my story, I get healed even further. I actually do not know who receives the bigger blessing; the single moms listening to the Principles or me.

I could only start right where I was at, even if I was lonely and depressed. The Bible says in Genesis 26:12, **"In the middle of a famine, Isaac sowed a seed in the land. And in the same year he received one hundred times what he planted and the Lord rewarded him mightily."**
In his greatest time of need Isaac did not sit around and wait for someone to do something for him. He rose up in the midst of his circumstances and sowed a seed.

God also says that He will satisfy your needs when you sow a seed. Maybe you are in a dry, sun scorched desert land in this single mom life, and you have a lot of needs for your self and your children. Maybe it is just having the basics; food, clothing and shelter. Maybe you are lonely and isolated, and need some loving women friends to connect with. Maybe it is finances that you need. Whatever your need is as a single mom, the first thing to do is get your mind off of your self and help meet the needs of someone else today. Do not sit around feeling sorry for your self and having tea parties with Satan like I did. Go find someone else that you can minister to. It is astonishing to think there are other single moms out there in worse shape than you are. They need you, and what you have to offer; even if it is just your shoulder to cry on.

God is just waiting to bless you and your family in abundance. The seed that you sow into someone else actually finishes the blessing for you. The size of your harvest depends on the amount of your seed.

Make a decision today to turn your attention away from yourself, and focus on being a blessing to other people. A healthy single mom concentrates more on being a blessing than being blessed. Ask God to bring people into your path that you can bless, and be on the lookout for opportunities to share God with others.

1. **Describe some ways you could be a blessing to others in your daily life.**
2. **What are some needs that you have personally? Who can you sow a seed into first to finish the blessings?**
3. **What is a hardship or pain from your life that you could comfort/minister to others? How can you serve others from this?**

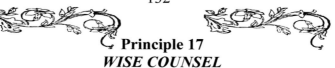

Principle 17
WISE COUNSEL

"Listen to counsel and accept discipline, that you may be wise the rest of your days. Proverbs 19:20

I was confused and disoriented when I became a single mom. Never have I been in a position where I absolutely did not know what to do in so many areas of my life. As you may recall from the other Principles, I suffered severe depression, and had a hard time just handling basic life. I lost my family, home and finances. I also found myself in a court system fighting for my son. My credit score went down the tubes, for I could not pay all of the debts that I "inherited" from the divorce. My life was unraveling right in front of my eyes, and I did not know what to do. Out of sheer desperation, I had to find someone to ask, "What should I do?"

My story reminds me of the widow in 2Kings 4:17 that says, **"Now a certain widow cried out to Elisha, "Your servant my husband is dead, and you know that your servant feared the Lord; and the creditor has come to take my two children to be his slaves." Elisha said to her, "What shall I do for you? Tell me, what do you have in the house?" And she said, "Your maidservant has nothing in the house except a jar of oil." Then he said, "Go, borrow vessels at large for yourself from all your neighbors, even empty vessels; do not get a few. "And you shall go in and shut the door behind you and your sons, and pour out into all these vessels, and you shall set aside what is full." So she went from him and shut the door behind her and her sons; they were bringing the vessels to her and she poured. When the vessels were full, she said to her son, "Bring me another**

vessel." And he said to her, "There is not one vessel
more." And the oil stopped. Then she came and told
the man of God. And he said, "Go, sell the oil and pay
your debt, and you and your sons can live on the rest."

I can relate to how this poor widow must have felt. She
just lost her husband, and everything she had to her name.
The creditors were coming to take her sons away, and the
only possession she had left was a jar of oil. She was wise
enough to seek out Elisha and ask, "Man of God what
should I do?" His advice and her actions blessed her for
the rest of her life. In this Principle we will explore what
the widow did, and how to apply this scripture to our lives
today.

1. She sought out Elisha.

This widow was in trouble, and she knew it. Her husband
passed away, and they were left with enormous financial
debt. The creditors were threatening to take her children
away to slavery to pay for these debts. She knew she
needed wisdom and guidance on how to handle this
situation. So what did she do? She sought out after Elisha,
the wisest man that she knew.

As a single mom, she did not try to figure out the answer
on her own. She is the one that went and sought out Elisha.
This is a biblical principle as Proverbs 4:1 says, **"Hear, O
sons, the instruction of a father, and give attention that
you may gain understanding."**

The widows husband was a prophet, and Elisha was the
over seer of her husband at the time he was alive. He was
also considered a father to the sons of the prophets. One of
Elisha's foremost concerns was for the welfare of these
families. Part of being an over seer is to be familiar with
the welfare, position and circumstances of families.

The Bible is filled with scripture that we are to have wise counselors and mentors in our life. Every single mom needs to seek these people out. She needs someone to pray for her, lean on, get guidance from and bounce ideas off of. We need mentors and wise counsel, especially with the overwhelming burdens we have, and the vulnerable position we may be in raising children alone. We also need them to help us develop spiritually.

When the Lord put on my heart that I needed wise counselors in my life my first thought was, "I do not know anyone like that." All I knew to do was pray about the situation. The Lord answered my prayer and put a certain couple on my heart from church. I admit I was distressed for I hardly knew these people, and they were not someone I would have initially chosen. I was also extremely intimidated by this situation, and even embarrassed to approach them. They were, however, elders in my church so I felt comfortable about that. I was still reluctant to go and talk to them. I thought they might reject me or think I was crazy in talking to them about this.

What I was most afraid of was exposing my self, my life, my past, and becoming vulnerable to people I hardly knew. I finally got up the courage to ask them if they would consider mentoring me. After talking in length with them they prayed about it, and felt this was indeed the Lords will. As it turns out, this has undoubtedly been the greatest blessing of my life.

As I mentioned earlier, the Bible is full of verses about the need of wise counselors in your life. Below are some scriptures about this from the book of Proverbs:

Proverbs 4:1
"Hear O sons the instruction of a father, and give attention that you may gain understanding."

Proverbs 8:33
"Heed instruction and be wise, and do not neglect it."
Proverbs 11:14
"Where there is no guidance, the people fall, but in abundance of counselors, there is victory."
Proverbs 12:15
"The way of a fool is right in his own eyes, but a wise man is he who listens to counsel."
Proverbs 19:20
"Listen to counsel and accept discipline, that you may be wise all the days of your life."
Proverbs 20:18
"Prepare plans by consultation and make war by wise guidance."
Proverbs 24:6
"For by wise guidance you will wage war, and in abundance of counselors there is victory."

I hope that you understand how serious God is about wise counsel, and that you must take the first step of action to seek it.

2. She shared her problem with him.
   The second thing the widow did was share her problems openly, and in detail with Elisha. She told him everything she was facing, and was transparent about how grim the situation was. The Bible says in Galatians 6:2, **"Bear one another's burdens, and thereby fulfill the law of Christ."** No single mom is an island. We should never think that we can be totally independent of others, or that we do not need help from anyone else. The body of Christ is required to work together for the common benefit of others.
   Please do not believe the lies that someone will judge you because of the difficult situations you face as a single mom.

If this couple is truly the wise counsel that God has for you, they will mentor you out of compassion and love; not judgment. In order to get the right advice and guidance you need, it is vital to share the entire situation with them. Do not leave any detail out or change the story in any way.

3. She was true to herself.

Wise counselors must be honest with you, and speak from truth and love no matter how much it hurts. It is essential they always tell you the truth, and lead you to the word of God. Do not choose someone that will only tell you what you want to hear. They need to be able to ask you the tough questions. Their wish should always be what God wants for you, not what they want for you or what you want for yourself.

Anyone not willing to tell you what you need to hear, because they knew you would not listen, is not a wise mentor. Their job is to always tell you the truth, and then you are responsible for what you do with it. You have the option to accept it or reject it. The point is that they must speak the truth no matter what the consequences of your actions are.

At times when my mentors tell me truth, it takes me a couple of days to genuinely process the information. This was especially true when we first started our relationship because I was clueless about the word of God. I promise it gets easier to accept their wisdom the more you know God's word on your own. (Thank you for your patience Bob and Marilyn!)

4. She was obedient to what he directed her to do.

Wise counsel will always guide you to do what God's word says to do. When the Lord introduced this Principle to me I was in an exceedingly fragile state of mind. It was crucial that I genuinely listened to what Bob and Marilyn were saying, for I knew they are instructing me from God's word. I had to make some tough decisions, and there was a lot at stake for my son and myself. At times, I had several choices for the solution to a problem I was facing. It was imperative that I made the right decision. Your job is to get advice from your wise counsel, and then use discernment about what to do with it. You are the only one responsible for your actions. After you make your decision, you can not go back to them and say they gave you poor advice. They are responsible to God to give you wisdom from the Bible, and you are responsible to God for what you do with it. I found that fasting is essential before making a key decision. If you do not know the answer wait before making a decision! Fast and pray some more to seek the Lord's will.

5. She held herself accountable to him.

The widow held herself accountable to Elisha to do what she was instructed to do. He told her to go borrow vessels; shut the door behind her and pour the oil. When the oil stopped pouring, she came back to Elisha. He then instructed her to go and sell the oil, pay her debts, and live off of the rest of the money. We always need to follow up with our wise counsel about our actions. It is necessary to have a plan for reality checks, for this helps us to stay on the straight and narrow path. Remember, the enemy's goal is to create distractions that will get you off track from accomplishing God's plan.

Instructions for a safe mentoring relationship.

I believe it is important to have a godly couple for mentors. In order for this relationship to work properly, guide lines are essential to have, and adhere to. All of you must be on the same page about the areas below. Feel free to bring this book with you when meeting potential mentors, and explain that these are your personal guidelines to follow. This will convey to them that you are extremely serious about what you are doing. It will also let them know that you are serious about protecting yourself, and their marriage. Do not be intimidated or waiver in any way about these rules. If for some reason they think any of them are trivial or unnecessary, they are not the right mentors for you.

1. Pray and fast about whom God would have as mentors for you before you approach anyone.

God knows exactly who your mentors are, and they may not be who you would have initially chosen. I believe they must also pray and fast as a couple before giving you an answer. This is an extremely serious relationship, and you need to make sure you are not working off of your feelings in any way. I never dreamed that Bob and Marilyn would be my mentors. I barely knew them, and I had some other people in mind that I really thought I should do this with. Thankfully I took the time to fast and pray to hear what the Lord had to say. I actually fought his answer for a while, and tried to make some of the other relationships happen. God was good though and made it impossible for those relationships to come about. He knew Bob and Marilyn were the right ones for me.

2. Always approach the wife first.

It is imperative that you take all precautions to keep every facet of the potential relationship, and their marriage safe. Approach the wife first and tell her exactly what you are trying to accomplish. Let her talk to her husband about it, and then get back to you. They must agree as a couple first that this is God's will. If one of them is not sure or does not agree, they are not the right mentors for you.

3. Always meet when they are together as a couple.
Never meet or talk to the man alone, or a one on one basis. Your job is to protect your reputation, and their marriage. Do not give anyone reason to question or doubt your actions. It is my practice to never be alone with a married man in any way. For example, perhaps you are going over to their house to meet, and for some reason the wife is not home yet.   Politely remind the man of your practice not be alone with a married man. Go back to your car and remain there until she comes home. This is extremely serious business ladies, for it is far too easy for a good situation to go wrong. I will never ride in a car alone with a married man or be in any situation that it would just be the two of us. Billy Graham would not even ride in an elevator one on one with a woman. He would wait for the next elevator that was empty or filled with people. That is how serious he is about protecting his reputation. You should be that serious also. If I have to meet any of my male business associates that are married, we always meet in a public restaurant and I have a third party with me. I also make sure their wives know that we are meeting. Is this drastic? Absolutely! I will not do anything that would make someone doubt my character or reputation, even if it means taking drastic measures.

4.   Establish ground rules first.
   The wife should be the overseer of the relationship, and act as the go- between in any way with you and her husband. She should always be your primary source of communication. If for some reason you do want or need to talk to the man, *always* get permission from the wife first to

contact him. She should also be the one to make the arrangements for you to communicate with him.

5. Any communication with the man should include the wife.

They may have their own system set up such as the wife always has a view of his emails. Protect yourself though, and if you email him, copy her on the email. If you text him, forward her the text. If you have a phone conversation with him, follow up with the wife immediately afterwards to let her know how the conversation went, and what you talked about. When you are in a group of married people, do not have an isolated conversation with a married man. Do every thing you can to include the wife or other people in the conversation with you. Again, I know this may seem extreme, but it is necessary for your own safety. Many single moms feel the wife is intimidated about a relationship with her and her husband. By following these guidelines, you and your children will be able to have healthy, long lasting relationships with other couples.

6. Pray for a Spirit of Unity.

When I need advice from my mentors, I ask the Lord for a Spirit of Unity. When I share something with them, I do not tell them what I think the answer is or what I thought I heard the Lord say. I share the details and facts, and then allow time for them to pray about it. When we meet again, if we do not have the same conclusion or word from the Lord, I wait before I act, and we pray again. The Lord tells us exactly what to do. It is remarkable to me that God tells both Marilyn and I the exact same thing; even down to specific numbers and details.

7. Hugs are from the side and an arms length away.
One of the many things I appreciate about mentoring with
Bob is the hugs I get. They are very "safe" hugs which
means they are off to the side with a distance between us.
This is not rude, it is safe and I truly appreciate it. I know
that he is protecting and honoring his marriage, wife, and
me. Even though they are not bear hugs, they are hugs of
love and respect. He would never put himself or me in an
awkward position physically. If anyone ever does put you
in a position like this, leave quickly and do not go near
them again. As I mentioned earlier, it is too easy for
something to go wrong, especially when you are vulnerable
both emotionally and physically. Again, go through each
of these guidelines with potential mentors. This will put
most everything out in the open, and establish safe rules for
everyone involved.

I am confident that you will enjoy this journey with the
wise counselors and mentors God has for you. It will take
some courage on your part to seek these people out, and
follow the guidelines above. By now you should trust that
God is with you, and that he wants nothing but the best for
you and your children.

1. What benefits do you think wise counselors would
    bring to your life?
2. What wrong roads could have been avoided by
    having wise counselors?
3. What areas would you want to hide from wise
    counselors? Why?
4. Think of three couples that are possible mentors?
    Pray, fast and commit a date to have wise
    counselors in your life.

Principle 18
COMMUNITY

"On the contrary, it is much truer that the members of the body which seem to be weaker are necessary." 1 Corinthians 12:22

Three enormous lies that I bought into when I became a single mom were, 1) I did not have a "family" anymore. 2) I did not fit in at my church anymore. 3) I was a "third wheel" around married people. All of these thoughts go against anything the Bible has to say about fellowship. God created us to be part of his family as Ephesians 1:5 says, **"He predestined us to adoptions as sons through Jesus Christ to Himself, according to the kind intention of His will.** When we accept Jesus Christ as our Lord and Savior, God becomes our Father. His children and the church then become our Spiritual Family. That divine family includes all believers past, present and future.

As you know, there are many ways that our families can be broken up. Our spiritual family, which is our relationship with all believers, is a family that will remain on all throughout eternity. Hopefully our physical family will be included in our eternal family.

I remember times when my Pastor would call husbands, wives and their children up to the alter and pray over them as a family. I would go not up there with my son because I felt like I did not have a family anymore in being a single mom. The Bible says in Matthew 12:48-50, **"Who is My mother and who are My brothers? And stretching out His hand out toward His disciples, He said, "Behold My mother and My brothers! For whoever does the will of My Father who is in heaven he is My brother and sister and mother."** After reading this verse, I realized my real family is not just my physical family; it is also my spiritual family in the body of Christ. Now that I am the Spiritual Leader of my home, I understand that I still do have a family. I have a beautiful child, my extended physical family, and an eternal family.

Becoming a member of God's family is the greatest joy, honor and privilege I have ever known. What else could compare with a family that will live on forever in paradise? Do you remember in the Principle of Identity, we learned to live off of truth, belief, behavior and feelings? Whenever you do not "feel" like you have a family as you once knew it, Gods word says that you do. As single moms, we need to recognize the *truth* that you are still a family. We need to *believe* that our true family is our spiritual family. We need to *behave* what we believe by gathering with other believers. Then we will *feel* like we belong, even when the circumstances may not seem like it.

Nowhere in the Bible does it say that I do not fit in anywhere at church because I am a single mom. That is a tactic of the enemy to keep you away from your spiritual family, and keep you isolated. We are called to belong to our spiritual family, not just believe in Jesus Christ. I know far too many single moms who profess to be Christians, yet choose to stay at home on Sunday mornings and watch church on TV. Your living room is not your spiritual home! We can get so far embedded in the lie that we do not fit in anywhere, we totally isolate ourselves from other believers.

The Bible says in Romans 12:4-5, **"For just as we have many members in one body and all the members do not have the same function, so we, who are many, are one body in Christ, and individually members one of another."** In this scripture Paul uses the analogy of a human body to teach Christians how we should live and work together. Just as parts of the body function under the direction of the brain, we as single moms and Christians are to work together under the power and authority of Jesus Christ. God gives each one of us gifts to build up His church, and he expects us to use them.

The Bible says in 1Corinthians 12:21-25, **"And the eye cannot say to the hand, "I have no need of you"; or again the head to the feet, "I have no need of you. On the contrary, it is much truer that the members of the body which seem to be weaker are necessary; and those members of the body which we deem less honorable; on these we bestow more abundant honor, our less presentable members become much more presentable, where as our more presentable members have no need of it. But God has so composed the body, giving more abundant honor to that member which lacked, so that there may be no division in the body, but that the members may have the same care for one another."**

The Bible emphasizes the importance of each church member regardless of marital status. If a part of it is taken away, the whole body becomes less effective. God created you for His purpose, and gave you gifts and talents that he wants you to use to glorify him in His church. You are a vital part of the body of Christ during this season of being a single mom, and so are your children. Whether you know it or not, your family has so much to offer your church. That is why it is a lie that you do not fit in there. If you feel that your church does not welcome you find one that does. Do you remember from the Principle of Communion, the four parts of being in Gods will? One of them was being an active part of God's Church.

God requires us to use the gifts that He gave us, and we are to encourage others to use theirs also. Get plugged in at church and do what God has asked you to do. Use the gifts and talents He has given you for His Glory. Stop the tea parties with Satan, get out of isolation and enjoy the pleasure of your church family. This is a great time to use your five fat files to see where you may be able to use your gifts and talents in the church.

God created us for relationships. We are designed for a relationship with God and other believers. It was so easy to think that I was just a "third wheel" when I was with other couples. The Bible says in Romans 14:19, **"So then, we pursue the things which make for peace and the building up of one another."** God wants us to focus on the things that we have in common, not the differences that we have. What are the things that a single mom and married couples have in common? Do you remember from the Principle of the Wedding, that you do have a husband? You are the Bride of Christ, and you are a mother. The only difference is that you have one husband; you're Heavenly Husband. They have two; their Heavenly Husband and their earthly one, and some of them would gladly trade places with you.

God created us all different and we should appreciate those differences. As single moms, we need to stay focused on what God wants for our lives; harmony as believers and loving others as Christ loves us – regardless of our marital status.

I made a decision to get to know at least three families in my church. I approached them to say they were a family that my son and I would like to get to know, and asked them if they would consider spending some time with us. They were thrilled, and we started out by having lunch together after church. That led to having meals together in each others homes which has led into friendships that I believe will last a lifetime. (Please follow the same guidelines in "Principle 17" for fellowship with other couples.)

You are not a second class citizen in any way because you are a single mom. You need other people and families, and they need you. The best thing you can do for your self and your children is to be around other strong Christian families. This will be a terrific gift to your children for the future as they get married and start their own families.

1. In what way do you feel less than a family?
2. What are some areas at church you can get plugged into?
3. Think of three families you would like to spend time with and make a plan to meet with them.

Note: "Purpose Driven Life", Rick Warren

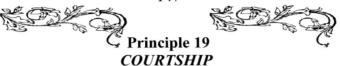

Principle 19
COURTSHIP

"If you do well, will not your countenance be lifted up? And if you do not do well, sin is crouching at your door; and its desire is for you, but you must master it." Genesis 4:7

My heart was pounding as I answered the phone. He was calling to let me know that he was only ten minutes away from my house. As I made some last- minute preparations with my hair and make up, I felt a warning signal from the Holy Spirit. Still, I added a little extra perfume that he liked so much down the length of my neck.

I can handle this I thought. After all, I have prayed real hard that I will not allow anything to happen tonight that shouldn't. As I stared at the clothes in my closet wondering what I should wear, again I felt a warning from the Holy Spirit. I did not tell anyone that I started seeing this guy or that he was coming over to my house.

I had a brief talk about him with one of my friends, and she determined from our conversation that he had a spirit of lust about him. I did not see it though for I was so thrilled that he called me at least three times a day, and we had some terrific conversations. He seemed genuinely attracted to me, and it sure did feel gratifying to have someone appear to be crazy about me.

The phone rang again. He said he just turned into my sub division. I quickly chose the conservative pants and sweater thinking that would eliminate the impure thoughts I had. I felt the nudge of the Holy Spirit again warning me that this was dangerous. I kept telling myself that I could handle this. After all, I am a grown woman, and I have my boundaries. I did not need to tell anyone about this because nothing was going to happen. As I saw the headlights of his car pull into my drive way, the thought came into my mind that we should not stay at my house. We should go out to a public place and not be alone like this. He was just way too cute, and I was much too attracted to him. Perhaps I was only attracted to the way he seemed so crazy about me. I was not quite sure what I was doing with this man or why I was having him over. I remember feeling terribly lonely at the time I decided to start seeing him. I did not see the "set up" that was right in front of me from the enemy.

Again I ignored the Holy Spirit's warning, for I had prayed the Lord's protection over me during this evening. I thought for sure that praying would keep me safe. When I heard the doorbell ring, I quickly turned on the stereo to my favorite jazz station, took one last look in the mirror and opened the door with a smile.

It was over with the moment I saw his face and let him walk through my door. No praying before hand was going to take care of the situation. I did not act responsible, and I never should have been alone with him. I just offered an open invitation for the enemy to walk right into my house. I did not follow principles and guidelines that I knew I should have. At the time I was weak, vulnerable and lonely as a single mom. I set myself right up to fall right into the arms of temptation.

As single moms, we have no business out running around with a man just so we can feel better about ourselves as women. We must be living out the reality of the Principle of the Wedding, that God is our husband. Remember that He does not want you to have an affair on Him!

I had to learn new methods to keep myself safe and pure, for the Bible says that **"Sin is crouching at your door."** Do you have any concept how serious the word "crouching" is in this verse? It means that the enemy is waiting to pounce on you with any opportunity you give him to come into your life. His goal is to kill you, steal from you and destroy you and your children. Getting into relationships that we do not belong in is the greatest realm where I believe Satan works in the life of a single mom.

When I opened the door to let that man into my house, sin was crouching at my door. The Bible says in 1Peter 5:8, **"Be of sober spirit, be on the alert. Your adversary, the devil, prowls around like a roaring lion, seeking someone to devour."** I invited sin with a red- carpet entrance into my house believing that I could handle this situation alone. I was also foolish enough to think that just because I prayed before hand that nothing would happen.

It is extremely selfish to have a sexual relationship outside of marriage. You defile, degrade and demoralize the man you are using to satisfy your own lustful desires. Next, you bring sin into your house that affects your children. You abuse the body God gave you, and you degrade and demoralize your self. You also ruin your reputation and integrity. That is exactly what Satan would want to happen to you.

The beautiful gift of sex that God made for marriage is the greatest weapon that Satan tries to use against us. It has destroyed me, along with numerous other single moms. God is a gracious God though, and he can take away all of those sins and restore you to back to full purity.

As women and responsible single mothers, we need to take some drastic measures to make sure that we keep ourselves pure and our children safe. For me, and I pray for you too, that means going back to some old fashioned courtship principles.

As you may recall from the Principle of the Wedding, I did not know what intimacy meant. The only intimacy I had ever known in my life was all physical. I felt led by

God to make this Principle of Courtship similar to the
Principle of the Wedding, and that means "Intimacy
without a physical touch" from a man during a courtship.
I have to admit that initially I could not understand how to
do this. I knew that I was being challenged by God not to
experience anything physical with a man until my wedding
day. This would allow me to understand true intimacy by
developing a deep friendship first, and not relate the
relationship to anything physical or sexual.

Satan uses sex as a way to blind us from the truth of what
the relationship or person is genuinely about. It is so easy
get caught up in our fleshly desires that we fail to see the
real truth about another person's nature and motives.

I am God's Bride and I need to make sure that I keep my
position with him pure. By doing this I am honoring God,
and the man I am involved with. This also helps to keep
my son and my home safe and secure.

There are three key guidelines that a single mom needs to
have in place if she is entering into a courtship.

1. She must be surrounded by her wise counsel and
    friends in her church that will advise and support
    her through out this time.
2. She must be content with God as her husband, and
    thoroughly enjoy being just with Him right now.
    She must love God deeply with all her heart, mind
    and soul, and know that she is whole and complete
    in Him and Him alone. She will seek to honor God
    throughout this courtship.
3. She must first have a strong friendship with this
    man before she becomes interested in him
    romantically.

So what does an old fashioned courtship look like? Dating is *not* for mating. It is for gathering information to see if this man is even worthy of your time. A season of courtship is to discover if God would genuinely want you to marry this man, and it should be a glorious time for you and this man to deepen your friendship. It is imperative to learn about each others character, morals, and values, and interact on a spiritual level with one another. It is a time to ask a lot of questions and grow closer to each other. All while refraining from physical intimacy.

Single moms can be so desperate to be married that we may settle for what ever man comes our way. We can also easily get thrown off course of the 21 Principles that God wants us to be following right now. In the difficult situations we face as single moms it is not easy to determine on our own if we are spiritually, emotionally and even physically ready for marriage. I have put some guidelines in my life that I take extremely seriously if I were to become involved with a man again. They may seem rather drastic at first but it is my responsibility to protect my relationship with God, and keep my self, my son and home safe. Below are my new rules for dating.

1. He will have to ask my mentor's permission to court me.

The correct way for a courtship to begin is for the man to approach my wise counsel and ask their permission to court me. What I will say to a man if he wants to see me is, "If you want to see me, you need to go see them first!" I can hear you saying, "What! She is a grown woman for Pete's sake." I promise that doing this will help you avoid so many mistakes. If I had a system in place when that man started calling me three times a day, I would never have become involved with him in the first place. If a man is not willing to go through this process, he is not someone to waste your time with.

I believe that as a woman and mother all alone, I need protection. I am reminded again of the scripture in 2 Timothy 3:5 where Paul is telling us what manner of men to stay away from; **"The kind that worm their way into households and captivate weak women."** I am well aware that at any given time I could be vulnerable. The real truth is that I do not always entirely trust myself.

One of the great privileges of being a man is the God given role as servant protectors and leaders. As we talked about in the Principle of Hope, perhaps your relationship with your earthly father was not the kind God meant it to be. You were never meant to be unprotected, left vulnerable, abused or mistreated in any way. One of the roles of the local church is to be the spiritual family that can step in for us where our biological family may be lacking.

I am honored that I have to two exceedingly wise men that love and care for both me and Eric. They will help me clarify, process and discern if this is even the right time for me to start a courtship. It will also help me see if indeed this is the right man for me based off of my desires in a husband. They both know where I am at spiritually, emotionally and mentally.

If this man actually has the courage to call my mentors and meet with them first, he will be met at their door with a shot gun. My mentors are here to make sure this person knows they are serious about protecting me. If he makes it through the door and actually talks with them, they are going to find out a lot about him in their conversation. (I would love to be a fly on the wall) Would you agree with me this will keep the "losers" away from you? These wise men will want to know about his salvation, what church he attends, who is pastor is, and who his wise counselors are. They will also learn about his children and his relationship with them. They will examine his character and discern any red flags I should be aware of. If he makes it to the next round, where we all spend time together, they will observe extremely close how he interacts with me, my son and his own children.

2. I will be accountable to them in every area.
   I need to guard my heart if I move into a courtship. I want to take the high road in every area of this relationship. I also need to understand that if this relationship is not the Lord's will for my life that is alright. I have not failed, and the relationship did not fail. It was just not the Lord's will with this man, and no one has been hurt or devastated. We can both walk away knowing we honored God.
   The main point of the courtship, as I mentioned earlier, is to "explore" if this is the right man for marriage. What I cannot do is dive head first into the relationship expecting it to turn into marriage, and then be crushed from false expectations if it does not. I have to take things slow and be patient as God unfolds His plan through out this time.
   There is no need to rush this relationship along. Impatience causes you to by pass the friendship phase, and move directly into emotional and physical intimacy. This is exactly why you must experience intimacy without a physical touch. How many times have you met someone and ended up talking all night long sharing your most personal matters? Conversations like that launch a relationship into high gear. You can become so emotionally attached that you miss the time it takes to cultivate a friendship or see what this person's character is truly all about. He does not need to know every thing

about you in one conversation. Emotional attachments are exceptionally strong for women, and this is where we tend to get hurt quickly. That is what guarding your heart is about; unfold a little at a time when and only if the time is right.

I always want to regard this man with nothing less than brotherly love. I need to see him as a brother in Christ, and not as a husband to me or a father to my son yet. This is not a time to play house or fantasize about marriage and the future. It is a time to gather information and build a strong friendship. It is wrong, and completely unfair, to put this person in a position that they are not yet meant to be in. It is also extremely unfair to your children .

The notion of love and passion can be exhilarating. If not handled correctly, the thrill can be over with in a moment and leave you with your head spinning; almost like a roller coaster ride. You are left wondering what the heck just happened in such a short amount of time.

Take the time to build a solid friendship before there is any divergence towards emotional or romantic intimacy. It should not take more than three dates to know if this guy is even marriage material. **If you have any doubts or see any red flags, get out of it quickly.** Too many times I see single moms essentially disappear from church when they get involved with a man. One single mom in a 21Principles class told me that at her age she was not going to pass up a date if someone asked her out. Sure enough, she started dating someone and fell away from her class. It turns out that she was doing this mans laundry and taking care of his children almost full time. Sadly, she found out he was seeing someone else at the same time. She came back to her 21Principles class several months later and needed tremendous healing all over again.

All of that could be avoided if we keep ourselves safe by going out with other couples and friends. This way, you can see what the other person is truly about in real-life terms. Your friends can also give you a better perspective on this guy from what they observe. Isolation in any way is dangerous and should be avoided at all times.

I believe it is imperative that I always tell my wise counsel where I am going and what I am doing with a man. No, this is not babysitting; it is protection for everyone involved. Remember, **sin is crouching at your door** just waiting to get you alone or off track in some way. If you ever feel that you cannot tell someone where you are going or what you are doing, it is something that you should not be doing.

I have a system set in place that someone will know where I am going and when I expect to be back if I am with a man. I will email them when I get home and "report in" that I adhered to *my own principles.* Remember, this is not about them. It is about you keeping your relationship with the Lord pure along with protecting yourself and your children. Always remember that God does not want you to have an affair on Him.

I will not go to a man's house to be alone with him, nor will I ask him over to my house. The temptations and dangers are great and much too serious. Yes, you need time alone but only under the proper conditions. These are reality checks to be accountable for. We need to make sure that we are always seeing the complete picture of what is happening in the relationship. It is too easy to get caught up in fantasies, illusions or get off track from the original intent in any way. That is why it is necessary to have other people involved with this courtship. We are called to be a holy people, not holy individuals. You should *never* proceed with a courtship alone. You need the body of Christ to celebrate with you, and hold you accountable to all areas of your life.

3. My first kiss will be at the alter.

I know how serious the Lord was that day when He said, "Don't you have an affair on me." I have decided that my first kiss will be when my pastor says, "You may kiss your Bride." I know where my greatest temptations and sins have been in the past, and Satan knows exactly where my weaknesses are also. I refuse to provide the enemy any opportunity to raise his ugly head and destroy the perfect gift of the marriage bed that God has designed for me. I am forgiven and cleansed from my past sexual sins, and I have kept myself pure both mentally and physically for God, and my husband. That is a beautiful gift to give to your husband on your wedding night.

You may be wondering, "How do you know if you want to marry this man if you have not even kissed him?" Elizabeth Elliott answers that question remarkably in her book "Passion and Purity." She so eloquently asks, "How in the world can you tell you want to marry somebody just because you have kissed them?" I guarantee that if this is the mate God has designed for you, the kisses are going to be incredible.

Intimacy is not necessary right now. Does that mean that you are to ignore your passions and challenge that you have them? No, it means that you must control them instead of them controlling you. Let's look again at the last part of our verse in Genesis 4:7 that says, **"Sin is crouching at your door, and its desire is for you, but you must master it."**

The best way to master anything, and fight a war, is to use your sword of the spirit which is God's word. There are two scriptures that I believe describe what intimacy without a physical touch means. The first one is from Ephesians

5:3 that says, **"But among you, let there not even be a hint of sexual immorality or any kind of impurity, or greed, because these are improper for Gods holy People."** The other one is from Song of Solomon 8:4 that says, **"Do not arouse or awaken love until it so desires. "** God makes it exceedingly clear there is an appropriate time for physical intimacy, and that time my dear single mom is to be on your wedding night.

Along with applying scripture to our lives, we must put into position measures to prevent us from sexual temptation. You saw how stupid I was to think that if I just prayed real hard before I invited that guy over to my house I could resist temptation. We must first do our part and act responsible by following the guidelines of this Principle. Then, God will do his part to help keep our emotions under control, and establish ways out of temptation for us.

I think resisting sexual temptation is harder right now as a single mom than it has ever been before as a woman. I know what it was like to be married and be intimate physically. I know how enjoyable it is to have someone to sleep with you, cuddle up with and knit yourself with physically. Even if it is just on the couch watching a movie all snuggled up.

We cannot do anything to give the enemy a foothold in this area of the physical realm. Our true hearts desire should be to honor God with our bodies, and serve each other by keeping mentally and physically pure. I have personally committed that my physical activity will not go beyond holding hands and hugging until my wedding day. (That means *after* the wedding) I will follow the guidelines below, and be accountable to them because sin is crouching at my door. I will master it for God, myself, my son, my home and the man I am with. My rules to master sexual temptation are as follows:

I will not engage in caresses of any kind such as:
> Massages
> Applying oil or lotion to each others skin
> Touching or playing with each others hair
> Holding or cupping each others face
> Stroking of the skin in any way

I will not allow myself to cuddle:
> Being entangled together in any way either on a couch or other areas
> Lying down next to each other
> Tickling or wrestling of any kind

I will not spend large amounts of time alone with a man:
> I will not go to his home and be alone
> I will not be alone with a man in my house
> I will not spend time alone when in vulnerable states such as being tired, or when it is late at night.

I will guard my conversations by:
> Not talking about the future with him or others until the appropriate time
> Not making plans for the future or "dreaming ahead of what could be" until appropriate
> Not talking about our future physical relationship
> Not lusting after him verbally or allowing lust in my mind

I will keep appropriate in my actions by
> I will dress in a manner that will not distract a man
> Mentoring with wise counsel about my mind and thoughts of lust or physical intimacy

This is something that your mentors and wise counsel should have in their hand to hold you accountable to at all times. I also believe it is suitable for mentors to go through this with the man if they do agree to a courtship. It is an excellent way to learn how serious this guy is about honoring God, you and your children. If he does not agree to abide by your wishes, and serve you with a pure heart, have nothing to do with him. Also, if he does not have wise counsel and mentors to hold him accountable, have nothing to do with him.

I know this may be difficult for you to put in place in your life, and that it is quite radical. Then again, wasn't Jesus considered radical for going against the world's desires? This Principle is all about honoring God, yourself, your children and the man you are with. Remember that you are Gods Bride and Royal Priesthood. You deserve an earthly King, and your children deserve the best man possible as a father. This Principle will help you to never settle for anything less than God's best for both you and your children.

1. **If someone wants to see you, who will they have to see first?**
2. **Create a list of your own Principles and hold yourself accountable to them.**
3. **When will your first kiss be?**

Note: "I Kissed Dating Goodbye, "Boy Meets Girl", Joshua Harris

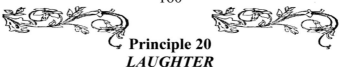

Principle 20
LAUGHTER

"In this you greatly rejoice, even though now for a little while, if necessary, you have been distressed by various trials, so that the proof of your faith, being more precious than gold which is perishable, even though tested by fire, may be found to result in praise and glory and honor at the revelation of Christ." 1Peter 1:6-7

The trials of being a single mom have been the most difficult ones of my life. I found myself in the position of being homeless, penniless and in court fighting a custody case for my son. I was also extremely overwhelmed from all I that I had to do. I often cried out to God saying, "Oh God, when is this hell on earth of being a single mom going to end? When will it ever get better? Just look at the situation I am in God. When am I going to come out of this mess?"

All I found my self doing as a single mom was focusing on my own living hell. All I could think of was me, my problems and how to get out of them. There was no joy, laughter or hope in my life at that time.

One night, the Lord's presence filled my room and He said, *"Lori, you will never be truly happy here on earth until you can learn to dance in the valley."* "What!" I said back to God. "Do you know what I'm going through now? Look at this life of mine. It stinks and this is not what I bargained for. I do not even know how I'm going to pay my bills. I hate being alone, and life is just a big gigantic mess. Yeah, I'm in the valley alright. Personally, I think it is the absolute pits, but if you like the word valley, I'll use that. The only thing I feel like doing is complaining right now, and the absolute last thing I feel like doing is dancing. You have got to be kidding God. It is just not possible to dance right now in this mess. This load is too heavy, and I am weighed down with so many burdens. I can not believe that you are asking me to dance in this situation. This is the pits, not a party. Dancing is for when you are happy, and frankly I am not smiling right now!"

The Lord said back to me, *"I know exactly how you feel. I felt the same way when I was beat, scourged and nailed to the cross. I do understand, and I want you to read the book of First Peter."* The book of First Peter is all about offering encouragement to suffering Christians, and how to share in the sufferings of Christ. Let me share a couple of verses with you that stood out to me as I read.

1Peter 1:6-7:
"In this you greatly rejoice, even though now for a little while, if necessary, you have been distressed by various trials, so that the proof of your faith, being more precious than gold which is perishable, even though tested by fire, may be found to result in praise and glory and honor at the revelation of Christ."

1 Peter 1:13:
"Therefore, prepare your minds for action, keep sober in spirit, fix your hope completely on the grace to be brought to you at the revelation of Jesus Christ.

1 Peter 2:21-23:
For you have been called for this purpose, since Christ also suffered for you, leaving you an example for you to follow in His steps, Who committed no sin, nor was any deceit found in His mouth; and while being reviled, he did not revile in return; while suffering, he uttered no threats, but kept entrusting Himself to Him who judges righteously.

1Peter 4:12-13:
Beloved, do not be surprised at the fiery ordeal among you, which comes upon you for your testing, as though some strange thing were happening to you; but to the degree that you share the sufferings of Christ, keep on rejoicing, so that

also at the revelation of His glory you may rejoice with exultation.

Seeing the word rejoice in the previous scripture made me think of the verse in Philippians 4:4 that says; **"Rejoice in the Lord always; again I say rejoice!"** I read somewhere that Biblical scholars thought when Paul wrote the book of Philippians that he was in a prison cell perhaps the size of powder room bathroom. It said the sewer went through or under the prison. Paul was more than likely on most occasions up to his waist in raw sewage while in prison. Do you feel that your single mom life is like being in a prison cell and you are in raw sewage up to your waist or higher?

Do you know what Paul did in his situation? He rejoiced, sang and possibly danced in the sewage. If he chose to rejoice, do you think that he *felt* like dancing in the sewage? My guess is more than likely not.

I said to the Lord, "I just do not feel like dancing. I have too many problems to deal with right now." All of a sudden a Holy Spirit alarm went off and reminded me that I was living off of my "feelings" instead of what God said to do. My mind went back to Principle #2 where I learned to live off of truth, belief, behavior, feelings. I heard God whisper to me again, *"Just dance Lori. Just give it a try."* Again, I found my self crying out to God saying, "I do not know how to dance when my whole life is falling apart right in front of my own eyes. Dancing just does not make sense in this situation." The Lord said back to me, *"I know, but remember, my ways are not your ways and my ways are higher than your ways. Just dance! Learn to dance in the valley."*

I was still extremely angry that God wanted me to dance. I thought it was the most ridiculous thing that I have ever been asked to do. "It just doesn't make sense" I kept telling myself. I love to dance, but only when I am happy. Dancing in the pits was not something that I could understand. I was still mad at God, and all I could think of doing was a little John Travolta, "Staying' Alive" move. "There" I said to God, "Are you happy now? I danced in the valley, and that is all I am going to do." God just said, *"Keep dancing. Dance in the valley."*

Well as you may know by now from the previous Principles, once God puts a word in my Spirit, it just does not let go of me. All I could think about was how to dance in the valley. I just wanted it to make some sense to me as to why I should do this. After a couple of days of torment, I felt led to go back to the verse in 1Peter 6-7 that says, **"In this you greatly rejoice, even though now for a little while, if necessary, you have been distressed by various trials, so that the proof of your faith, being more precious than gold which is perishable, even though tested by fire, may be found to result in praise and glory and honor at the revelation of Christ."**

The Lord spoke to me and said, *"Lori, you need to rejoice during this time. It is just a season, and my word says it will last only for a little while. But I see it necessary for you to be distressed right now, because Lori I want you to have a big faith, so I can bless you big. I need you to put your faith in me, not money or earthly things that you think are going to bring you out of this situation. Remember Lori, this is nothing but a test right now. It is not about your situation; it is about me! Life is about me! I want to promote you and take you to higher places, and the only way I can do this is to test you, and the only way you can get there is to pass the test. So Lori, do not be surprised that this test is upon you and act like some strange thing is happening. Remember my word in James* 1:**2 "Consider it pure joy when you encounter various trials, knowing**

that the testing of your faith produces endurance. And
let endurance have its perfect result, so that you may be
perfect and complete, lacking in nothing."** *In order for
me to give you what I want, I need to find you in Praise and
Glory. Keep on rejoicing, so that also at the revelation of
My glory you may receive exultation. Dance in the valley
Lori, Dance in the Valley."*

My dear Single mom, do you know what it means to
receive exultation? It means to be overjoyed and
triumphant. God wants us to be filled with His joy and be
victorious in all things.   The Bible says in John15:11,
**"These things I have spoken to you so that My joy may
be in you, and that your joy may be made full."**

It is so easy to praise God as a single mom when our
checking account is full and we can pay our bills. It is so
easy to say thank you and dance around when we have
what we need. But when the hardships are there we go
around whining and complaining. We get angry at God,
mad at the world, frustrated, depressed and ready to give
up. I know because I've been there. God does not want
our lives to be like a roller coaster; depressed and down in
the dumps because of our circumstances, and then on a
high the next. God wants you to be level headed at all
times, no matter how low the circumstances or how high
the good times are. Remember that Satan is the one who
wants you down in the dumps and depressed.

Let's go back to the verse in 1 Peter 1:13 that says,
"Prepare your mind for action, keep sober in spirit."
Do you consider depression and hopelessness being sober
in spirit? I think not! The Bible says in 1Peter 5:8, **"Be of
sober spirit, be on the alert. Your adversary the devil,
prowls around like a roaring lion seeking someone to
devour."** Satan wants us to live in defeat, and God wants
us to live in victory. When we dance and rejoice in the

worst of times we bop Satan right over the head with a big stick. Praise helps us keep our mind alert and of sober spirit. In other words, praise kicks the enemy right out the door.

As I mentioned earlier, I told God that I did not know how to dance in the valley, but I was ready to give it another try. All I could think of to do was just sway my body while singing, "I do not know how I'm going to pay my bills God, but I'll dance." The Lord said, *"That's good Lori, just keep dancing."*

I spent the next couple of weeks complaining first, and then dancing and praising. For some strange reason I felt like I wanted to add a little bit more into the song and dance God wanted me to do. I started twirling while singing and praising. None of my circumstances had changed yet, and I was not seeing any results in the natural from dancing in the valley. Little did I know that God was working behind the scene, and something was starting to move in the supernatural. All I heard was *"Keep dancing in the valley."* So I twirled and moved more around my living room while praising.

After about a week of this I started to feel a little foolish, and I'm sure I looked foolish also. I have to admit though I was starting to feel a little bit better. I was laughing a little bit and enjoying dancing around the room. I am not sure if that was because I had some of God's joy in me, or because I looked in the mirror and saw how silly I looked. I decided not to waste my time trying to figure out why I was having fun, and just enjoy the fun I was finally having.

Now my dancing in the valley went something like this, "I don't know how I'm going to pay my rent, and I'm scared. But I bless you Lord, I bless you Lord, I bless you Lord. Oh God, when are you going to change this situation? I have a stack of bills, my son needs things for school, gas prices are at three dollars a gallon. I hate being a single mom, and I wish you would bring me a husband. I bless you Lord, I bless you Lord, I bless you Lord."

I do not know how many weeks my dancing in the valley went on for like that. My circumstances had not changed, but I was feeling a little better than I did before.
I remember asking God one time, "How do you feel about me complaining first and praising you second?" He said for me to read the Psalms, for it was full of people like me telling God how they felt about the circumstances they were in. Then He directed me specifically to Psalms 3. David started out that Psalm complaining. It only took him to get to the third verse before he realized who he was complaining to; it was God. I kept hearing, *"Just keep dancing Lori. Dance in the valley."*

I still complained first and danced next knowing full well that there needed to be more to this than what I was doing. Suddenly, out of the blue I felt like reversing the direction of my dance. I started out with, "I bless you Lord, I bless you Lord, I bless you Lord. I don't know how I am going to pay my bills, but I bless you Lord, I bless you Lord, I bless you Lord." I am here to tell you, the next day something supernatural happened.   My spirit got filled with something that made me truly want to dance. I finally realized that I needed to put the praise first, and then tell God what I was dealing with. It all started to make sense now that praise needs to lead the way!

The more I praised first, and told God how I felt second, the more something kept rising up in my spirit. In the next couple of days, I started to feel stronger on the inside. My circumstances had not changed; yet something was changing inside of me. I started to laugh and smile again, and I even started looking forward to my day when I woke up.   There was genuinely hope now that just maybe everything was going to be alright.

I started to have so much fun that I added a little more praise into the dance like, "I bless you Lord, I bless you Lord, and I bless you Lord. I praise you Lord, I praise you Lord, I praise you Lord." The more I praised, the less I complained and focused on my problems and circumstances. When I started to praise more and complain less, my circumstances starting turning around. When I danced in the valley and gave praise to God first, I started to make a little more money. My depression started to lift; I started singing a little bit more and my son start singing too. I saw the enemy pack up and leave my house.

My dancing in the valley and signing praise, despite my difficult circumstances as a single mom, just gave Satan an eviction notice from my life and my house. I felt a peace in my home like I have never known before. The Lord started opening doors for me to minister to other single moms. Churches started calling and inviting me to come and speak, and I got paid doing it. The 21Principles CD's got taped and started to sell. The 21Principles DVD series got filmed and churches started using the 21Principles as small groups. My debts started getting paid off, and my personal finances started to turn around. I believe it was all because I learned to dance in the valley and let praise lead the way! My circumstances did not change until I changed. This lesson was not about my circumstances, it was about my attitude towards my situation.

Something also changed when I finally made it to the mountain top. You know that place where we usually jump around, throw our hands in the air and profess our victory. That place where we look down into the pit and say, "Ha! Look at me know! I made it out of there. I'm on top of the world now." It is the place where we normally experience the enormous adrenalin rush and major highs. The mountain top was not the same anymore, for it did not have the high rush to it like it used to. It was a delightful place to be though, for I could take a deep breath and relax a little bit. I finally realized that when you can learn to dance in the valley, it can be one of the happiest places in the world. That is the time when we are closest to God, and when we need him the most.

God's joy truly does become complete in you when you dance in the valley. It is the place where we as single moms truly experience God, and all of his goodness and glory. It is the place where there is nothing left to do but get out of our self and get into God.

You can be assured now that your valley is a place where God thought it was necessary for you to be at this time, so you could come out with a big faith in Him and not earthly treasures. Remember that God wants to promote you, and the only way he can do that is when you learn to dance in the valley.

My dance is so much different now than it was back then. I have come to realize that the real dance is praising God for who He is, and not ask anything of Him. That is the perfect dance.

My dance has gone from the rebellious "Staying Alive" move to dancing with my Father in a movement of grace. It is a dance of love now; a passion for Him, and to praise him for the Almighty God that He is.

When we learn to dance in the valley as a single mom, we praise God and worship Him for who He is and what He has done for us. It is a place where we learn to trust God, lay down our requests at his feet and walk away. God wants us to come out of this with a big faith in Him. As single moms, we need to stand firm on God's promises that He is who He says He is in the situation you are facing. If you need finances, praise Him that He is your Jehovah-

Jireh. If you need peace, praise Him as your Jehovah-Shalom. If you need healing, praise Him as your Jehovah Rophe. God is the great "I am," and what ever it is that you need, praise Him that he can fulfill it.

So my dear single mom, if you are in a trial today, "Rejoice in the Lord always, and again I say rejoice." It will only be for a little while, and God sees it necessary for you to be there. He wants you to have a big faith in Him, which is more precious than earthly treasures. Remember it is only a test.   All God genuinely wants to know is will you dance with Him in the valley? Will your true joy come from Jesus Christ alone?

It is my prayer that God will find you in praise and glory and honor at the revelation of Jesus Christ. So dance my dear single mom. Dance in the valley.

1. What is your current attitude in the valley or pits? Create a plan to "Dance."
2. What is your attitude about trials now knowing that God may see them necessary?
3. Compare Jesus' suffering to yours. Do you see your suffering in a different manner now?
4. What are you putting your faith in to get you out of the trial besides Jesus?
5. What will you do to be found in Praise, Glory and Honor at the revelation of Jesus?

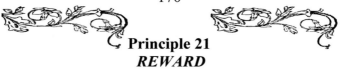

Principle 21
REWARD

"Her children will rise up and call her blessed" Proverbs 31:28

Can you believe that we are at the end of our 21 Principles? Even though it may be the end of the book, it is just the beginning of a life time to become the woman and mother God wants you to be in this season of single motherhood.

I know it has been a lot of hard work to renew your mind, and destroy old habits, and I am confident that you have done exceptionally well so far. I pray that you continue to grow deeper in God's word as you use these 21 Principles of a Healthy Single Mom in your life.

I am the type of person who writes notes all over my bible, especially when I hear a compelling sermon and when I study. Through all of my notes and color coded highlighted scriptures, there is one note in my Bible that I will treasure forever. My son wrote it in my favorite passage; Proverbs 31. Next to the verse that says, "Her children will rise up and call her blessed" my son wrote, "You rock Mom!" Now for some of you that might not seem remarkably spiritual. For me, it is the reward of everything that I have tried to live my life for; to be the best example of a woman who loves God to my child.

I have one main goal in my life as a mother and that is to raise a child with a heart after God. It is my responsibility to train my son up in the way of Lord, not the churches responsibility. I know that one day he will train up his children, and so on down the line of this generation. What you do with your children today effects every generation that follows.

One of my favorite books in the Bible is the book of Joshua. I look at my responsibility as a mother in almost the same way as the relationship between Moses and Joshua. The first two verses of Joshua say, **"Now it came about after the death of Moses the servant of the Lord, that the Lord spoke to Joshua the son of Nun, Moses' servant saying, "Moses my servant is dead; now therefore arise, cross this Jordan, you and all this people, to the land which I am giving to them, to the sons of Israel."**

There is going to come a time in my son's life when I am no longer on this earth. In a couple of years Eric will be living his own life and I will not have authority over him any more. My prayer is that I raised a God loving, responsible, courageous man.

Joshua was Moses personal assistant for forty years and succeeded Moses as Israel's leader. Because Joshua assisted Moses for so many years, he was well prepared to take over the leadership of the nation. Think of it, Joshua's new job was to lead more than two million people into a strange new land and conquer it.

What ever position God has for my son in the future, I pray that I trained him in the eighteen years or so that I had with him to be more than a conqueror. God's plan for our children may not be to lead nations. I do know that everyday our children face extremely difficult situations in this world, and have to deal with some evil people and wicked temptations. I pray that my son will be well equipped to face those situations, and deal with them based off of the word of God that he was taught at home. My son may not lead a nation, but he will lead his family one day and raise up a future generation. My job is to prepare him by the example that I am to him right now.

I taught Eric to be extremely brave and stand up to say no to drugs, alcohol, sex outside of marriage and all of the other crazy peer pressures that he will face. I taught him that God has a better plan for him that will bring him joy and success just like Joshua 1:7 says, **"Only be strong and very courageous; be careful to do according to all the law which Moses My servant commanded you: do not turn from the right or to the left, so that you may have success wherever you go."** It is my responsibility to mentor him in the way of the Lord, like Moses did for Joshua.

I remember sitting at my kitchen table unusually early one morning feeling extremely overwhelmed. There was so much to do for my son with school and sports. I always wanted to be the one to teach him all of these things. That dream seemed impossible now for I had to go back to work. I now had to rely on other people to do the precise things that I always wanted to do for my son. As I cried out to the Lord for help, I felt the Lord tell me that my job was to teach my son the word of God. If I did that He would take care of the rest. I did the best that I could in that area. As I look back on my son's life, I am so grateful for the teachers, coaches and other Godly people the Lord has brought into his life that are such a positive influence on him.

Whenever Eric and I do things together around the house, such as laundry, dishes and chores I tell him these are things that he will have to do as a husband or father. I try to let him in on the little things that his wife will appreciate him doing when he is married. One particular night Eric was complaining that he had to do chores. I used it as a teachable moment to tell him this is a fabulous way to spend some talk time with his wife when he is married, and how much she would appreciate that. I asked him what he thought his day would be like when he is a husband father.

His answer brought joy to my heart, and literally made my knees buckle.

Let me share with you what he described an "average" day would be in his family.

1. He would get up early in the morning before everyone else and pray and read his Bible.
2. He would pray with his wife as soon as she woke up and read God's word to her.
3. He would read the Proverb of the day to his family at breakfast.
4. He would pray with his children before they went to school.
5. He would read the Psalms to his family at dinner time.
6. He would read the children's daily reading with them at night.
7. He would pray with, and over his children before they went to bed.

Needless to say, I was elated to hear him say that at the age of ten years old. As I heard him describe his day, it dawned on me that is exactly what I do with him right now. I decided a long time ago to make these things a non-negotiable for myself and my son. I plan for these things in my day because I consider them an investment in my son's future and his character.

As I lay in bed that night pondering what I heard my son describe earlier, I wondered what would happen if he did not grow up to live like that? The Lord spoke to me again and assured me that I was not to think like that. He instructed me to meditate on Proverbs 22:6 that says, **"Train a child in the way he should go, and when he is old he will not turn from it."**

I believe the greatest reward of my life will be to see my son living out a godly life on his own. He has a free will though, and the choices he makes for his life are clearly his own. My prayer for him is to be filled with wisdom and discernment beyond his years, and knowledge of God's word to make "Blessable decisions."

I also thought about the conversations I had with Dr. Charles Stanley and Dr. John Trent as they spoke so fondly of their single mom mothers on the 21 Principles CD series. I wondered what my son would say about me when I am gone from this earth. How would he describe my life or what I meant to him? What would he tell his children about their Grandma? What kind of legacy will I leave in Eric? For me to hear him say, "She taught me the word of God" would make me the happiest woman ever. For right now though the words, "You rock Mom" are all that I need to hear!

I close this book with the scripture from Proverbs 31:30 that says, **"Charm is deceitful and beauty is vain. But a woman who fears the Lord, she shall be praised."**

1. **What would your children say about you if they were to describe your life?**
2. **How would they describe what you meant to them as a mother?**
3. **What do you think they would tell their children about you?**
4. **What kind of legacy are you passing down to your children?**
5. **What changes do you need to make in your life for the answers you really want to hear from these questions?**

If the 21 Principles have blessed you, please help me reach other single moms that need them also. Simply cut out the coupons on the next page and PASS IT ON !

HOPE & HELP
For The Single Mom
Order the Book Today at:
www.hope4singlemoms.com

HOPE & HELP
For The Single Mom
Order the book Today at:
www.hope4singlemoms.com

HOPE & HELP
For The Single Mom
Order the Book Today at:
www.hope4singlemoms.com

HOPE & HELP
For The Single Mom
Order the Book Today at:
www.hope4singlemoms.com

HOPE & HELP
For The Single Mom
Order the Book Today at:
www.hope4singlemoms.com

HOPE & HELP
For The Single Mom
Order the Book Today at:
www.hope4singlemoms.com

HOPE & HELP
For The Single Mom
Order the Book Today at:
www.hope4singlemoms.com

HOPE & HELP
For The Single Mom
Order the Book Today at:
www.hope4singlemoms.com

HOPE & HELP
For The Single Mom
Order the Book Today at:
www.hope4singlemoms.com

HOPE & HELP
For The Single Mom
Order the Book Today at:
www.hope4singlemoms.com